Steve Aylett:
A Critical Anthology

SEIN UND WERDEN / BOOKS

Steve Aylett: A Critical Anthology

Edited by Bill Ectric and D. Harlan Wilson

Special thanks to Rachel Kendall for
additional editorial assistance

SEIN UND WERDEN / BOOKS

http://www.kissthewitch.co.uk/seinundwerden/books.htm

Published in the United States of America
Jacksonville, FL: Sein und Werden/Books, July 2016
Library of Congress Control Number: 2016941532

ISBN-13: 978-0692717271
ISBN-10: 0692717277

CONTENTS

Uncanny Recognition

Bill Ectric

My first visit to Steve Aylett's mythical city of Accomplice was disorienting, like getting off a Greyhound bus in a strange town in the middle of the night. *Karloff's Circus* (2004) begins with Mike Abblatia preparing to jump to his death from the Jericho Bridge. In *The Complete Accomplice* (2010), Aylett writes: "He climbed into the black suspension girders and stood a while listening to the sizzle of night insects" (289). In the beautifully rendered opening of the book, three synchronous events unfold around this pivotal bridge in the twilight. First, we are walking on the bridge with Mike Abblatia. Then, as he plummets earthward, Karloff Velocet's mystery train roars into the picture, overhead, crossing the bridge. Karloff catches a glimpse of the falling figure's newly sprouted wings "gliding low and fast through the gloom" (289). Finally, while Barny Juno is visiting his parents the same night, he sees "a bunch of circus freaks chasing some sort of angel through the forest" (291).

One reason for my disorientation is that I started with the last book of Steve Aylett's four-book *Accomplice* series. This was before they were collected into one volume and I didn't know it was a series. Frankly, I chose *Karloff's Circus* because the title reminded me of Boris Karloff, the English actor who made a name for himself as the Frankenstein monster in the 1930s. But the main cause of my disorientation was unfamiliarity with Aylett's style, and to a lesser extent, with his characters.

People often forget that someone taught them much of the literary knowledge they now take for granted. Years ago, a tenth grade English teacher explained that Ray Bradbury's "thimble seashells" in *Fahrenheit 451* (1953) were ear pieces for listening to the radio, and that the fire truck was called a "salamander" because of an old superstition that salamanders could live in fire. These many years later, it is easy for me to assume that I knew those things from the beginning. As for style, it generally takes a few pages to acclimate myself to certain eighteenth and nineteenth century authors if I haven't read them in a while. Why should a new book necessarily be different? I remember struggling through Mary Shelley's *Frankenstein* (1818) when I was 12 years old. A few years later, when I read it again, a combination lock clicked open in my brain. So, in a way, getting familiar with Steve Aylett's style was like being a kid again. Comprehension is a marvelous sensation. It would not surprise me to learn that endorphins are involved. I'm told that even the act of smiling releases endorphins in the brain, and I certainly found myself smiling repeatedly as I acclimated to *Karloff's Circus*.

Once my pupils had adjusted to the Accomplice nightlife, I looked for signposts. Specifically, I sought the intersection of "satire" and "cyberpunk," two labels that appear frequently in reviews of Aylett's work. Aylett has said that if people must put his work in a genre, he would prefer the satire category (Taylor). When interviewed by Justin Taylor for *Bookslut*, Aylett said:

I like taking arguments or sound bites and taking them apart, or accelerating them to see where they lead. Satire takes an argument, exposes it to reality and feeds it back to the person who stated it. If it's got integrity they shouldn't be afraid of taking it in again. But if the argument is flawed, the satirical version will open out inside them like a complicated bomb and wreak a bit of havoc. This assumes that the person reading has an atom of honesty to appeal to, and that they're not so infected with postmodern evasion strategies that they can't acknowledge the existence of a factual world. (Taylor)

Aylett frequently cites Voltaire as a major influence, adding that he read *Candide* (1759) after receiving it as a gift from his father and it is one of his favorite books (Aylett, "Re: Beginnings"). To a lesser degree, he acknowledges Thomas Love Peacock, specifically in connection to *Bigot Hall* (1995), a novel that Aylett describes as his "attempt to re-establish, in a modern and more extreme way, a genre created by Thomas Love Peacock, an author I discovered in my early teens. In fact, some of the *Bigot Hall* material was written in my teens" (Taylor).

John Mair described the difference between Voltaire and Peacock by observing that "Dr. Pangloss [in Candide] required the Lisbon earthquake to illustrate opinions that Dr. Folliott [in Peacock's *Crotchet Castle* (1831)] would have expounded over the dinner table" (Mair 11-12). In fact, much of Aylett's work combines the bawdy, action-oriented style of Voltaire with the sedentary, faux cultivated style of

Peacock. For example, Aylett's *Atom* (2000) features a car chase in which brief descriptions of high-speed road maneuvers are sandwiched between chatty conversation among the drivers and passengers. On the outside, vehicles swerve and tires screech; inside, small talk and philosophical observations bounce around in noir-gangster parlance.

Aylett can write a deft action scene when he wants to. In *Novahead* (2011), the final Beerlight novel, he depicts an epic gunfight amongst rival gangs, the police, and "some kids who had probably been out playing real murder ARGs" or alternative reality games (39). All of the participants are in their element, like a Zen moment in a baseball game, relishing a continuum in the endless summer of gunfights.

> **Everyone was up and at it, running around and enjoying themselves. A burning squad car peeled off . . . fishtailing from side to side. Then it slowed to a stop, the driver emerging to roll around and beat at the flames, or perhaps he was energetically waving his arms and legs to communicate something he'd realised amid this extremity (42, 43).**

Aylett adds another dimension to the battle scene, literally, by superimposing an evolving geometric pattern over it. The chapter begins with a rectangle, represented by a garage doorway: "We stood before the swelling rectangle until the door grated into place above us. All I could see at first was a collision of dust clouds, and then the dim skeletons of cars" (38). Next, the various battling factions take cover at obtuse angles to one another, roughly forming lines. The lines, in turn, form shapes.

> **Jose came out of nowhere, trotting to a crouching halt behind the crinkled snout of the flipped cab. He wasn't our ally but of course he was versus the cops so he was happy to hunker nearby on our right but at a slight angle. The ARG kids were on our left behind a fallen gun shop billboard, also at a slight angle that satisfied their independence. Ideally, a complete circle would allow for everyone. Without the cops, our three emplacements could close to a triangle. The crappiest arrangement would be a square. Why? I pictured a conflict fractal, the same patterns repeated at every scale. (41)**

Fractal patterns emanating from a cube result in a hypercube, also known as a tesseract, which, in physics, represent the fourth dimension (time). British mathematician Charles Hinton coined the term "tesseract" in 1888 ("Tesseract"). Aylett often references Hinton in his books and in interviews. One could call the entire gunfight scene an example of pure science fiction, or more precisely, fiction written by someone who sees action unfolding in time as well as space. Perhaps a square would be the "crappiest arrangement" because, if the aforementioned repeating fractals continue unabated, the violence will escalate into apocalypse (41).

Another technique that is more in the style of Peacock than of Voltaire is Aylett's use of "lists" for humorous effect. These are not numbered lists; they appear in paragraph form, flowing non-stop as though from a wellspring, cataloguing an increasingly more absurd series of objects or concepts. In "Maryland," for example, a clergyman claims to see the shape of the Madonna in a pool of blood under the body of a murder victim. When a crowd grapples over the body, the blood puddle is disturbed and altered repeatedly, so as to resemble, in turn, "a monster truck, a flight bag, pond dice, inflatable hammers, a pig in a tire swing, an inarticulate outcast, a wily sheriff containing the answers, a map of Denmark, a camel, a weasel, a whale" (*Toxicology*).

Compare and contrast the above list to a passage in Peacock's *Headlong Hall*, where Squire Headlong prepares for the arrival of "his philosophical and dilettanti visitors," whom he hopes to impress by stocking his house with:

> **books, wine, cheese, globes, mathematical instruments, turkeys, telescopes, hams, tongues, microscopes, quadrants, sextants, fiddles, flutes, tea, sugar, electrical machines, figs, spices, air-pumps, soda-water, chemical apparatus, eggs, French-horns, drawing books, palettes, oils, and colours, bottled ale and porter, scenery for a private theatre, pickles and fish-sauce, patent lamps and chandeliers, barrels of oysters, sofas, chairs, tables, carpets, beds, looking-glasses, pictures, fruits and confections, nuts, oranges, lemons, packages of salt salmon, and jars of Portugal grapes.**

Humor is intended in both passages, but the humor in Peacock's list derives not so much from the quirkiness of the items listed but the sheer number of items, emphasizing the Squire's overly enthusiastic expectations. It could be argued that the "scenery for a private theatre" in Peacock's list does actually match Aylett's level of absurdity.

Aylett himself has said, "Lists and patterns are a way of loading a lot of information, or at least a lot of colors and textures, all of which also help to make a world solid through specific-rich detail" ("Re: Beginnings").

Some of the items in an Aylett list are specific references, while others are included either for their comedic effect or to paint impressionistic pictures. Readers need not recognize every reference to appreciate the prose. The non-sequiturs, hyperbole, unexpected juxtapositions, and sheer randomness are enjoyable enough in their own right. Karloff Velocet arrives in Accomplice and, with great fanfare, begins to introduce the acts and performers featured in his Circus of the Heart's Shell, proclaiming in *The Complete Accomplice*: "I bring you the disadvantages of bloody mayhem! Parlour tricks which have escaped my control! Shabby secrets ejected and at large! Resentful rarees and pointless oddities! Barbaric skull percussionists and bandaged fire bugs!" (292-93). And, as Velocet speaks, the following action unfolds: "Along the twisted rack of trailers carved with sigils and baffle-like creeper fluting, boilerplate doors flew off and a platoon of clowns surged into the square, bearing all the paraphernalia of their foul calling. Among them were freaks, tumblers, crumblers, and flamers" (293). The writing style in this passage (including the enumeration of circus acts) sets the tone of the action.

In a similar way the following excerpt from Peacock's *Nightmare Abbey* serves the same function and conveys the mood of the youthful and imaginative Scythrop:

> **He built many castles in the air, and peopled them with secret tribunals, and bands of illuminati, who were always the imaginary instruments of his projected regeneration of the human species... he slept with Horrid Mysteries under his pillow, and dreamed of venerable eleutherarchs and ghastly confederates holding midnight conventions in subterranean caves . . . immersed in gloomy reverie, stalking about the room in his nightcap, which he pulled over his eyes like a cowl, and folding his striped calico dressing-gown about him like the mantle of a conspirator.**

In addition to satire, I went into Accomplice looking for cyberpunk, and latched on to a passage in which the demon Sweeney tears himself away from his throne. Aylett says, "Sinews stretched, gas exploding from fluke-holes" (340), I told myself that the real world is no less freakish. Even today, there are people connected by tubes to machines, kept alive in hospitals against all laws of nature. Once we establish that our world is crazy, it makes no difference whether Aylett uses surrealism to parody reality or if he writes a straightforward story about paranormal creatures in a parallel universe. But what was I to make of the assortment of demons, clowns, factory workers, zombies, politicians, and giant Steinway spiders? The Steinway spiders immediately brought the works of

Salvador Dali to mind. Ominous clowns have become a staple of weird fiction. Karloff Velocet's train enters the town by bursting out of someone's mouth. Ultimately, then, the *Accomplice* series transcends metaphor and erupts into full-bloom metaphysical fantasy.

The cyberpunk genre is best represented in the Beerlight novels and stories, where many sentences offer multiple interpretations. Characters often light up and smoke "shock absorbers." Obviously, this could be a slang term for cigarette, like *stogie*, *coffin nail*, or *square*. Furthermore, a smoker might say cigarettes help them relax, or "take the edge off"—thus they are "shock absorbers." Taking it a step further (because a shock absorber is a large and bulky cylindrical apparatus), maybe it's a metaphor for an exceptionally large cigarette, cigar, or spliff. Characters speak of smoking *torpedoes*, *bombers*, and *trees*. Why not a *shock absorber*? Then we have a third interpretation, which is a surreal cartoon-like image of characters puffing on actual shock absorbers. Strange as that may sound, Aylett's Beerlight books give us enough other bizarre scenarios (e.g., guns with metaphysical ammunition and a talking piranha named Jed Helms) to spring our psychic floodgates open for anything. This all takes longer to write than it does to think about. One learns to roll with it. Sometimes I go for two or three pages before I absolutely have to stop, ponder, and appreciate an especially obscure passage, but that's part of the fun.

I am reminded of the following statement: "Two different people can read the books and seem to have read different books" ("Re: Beginnings"). No single interpretation is correct; this is fiction, after all. Jacques Derrida maintained that all words have varying shades of meaning to each reader; therefore, every reader brings a certain amount of the story with them to a book. Aylett gives us an abundance of raw materials to process.

Works Cited

Aylett, Steve. *Atom*. New York: Four Walls Eight Windows, 2000.

―――. *The Complete Accomplice*. London: Scar Garden Press, 2010.

―――. *Novahead*. London: Scar Garden Press, 2011.

―――."Maryland." *Toxicology*. 1999. London: Scar Garden Press, 2012. Kindle.

―――. "Beginnings." Message to Bill Ectric. 14 July 2013. Email.

Mair, John. "Introduction." *Three Novels: Headlong Hall, Nightmare Abbey and Crotchet Castle* by Thomas Love Peacock. 1940. Nashville: Thomas Nelson & Sons, 2008. 7-12.

Peacock, Thomas Love. *Headlong Hall*. 1815. Project Gutenberg. 2 July 2004. Ebook.

―――. *Nightmare Abbey*. 1818. Project Gutenberg. 19 Nov. 2011. Ebook.

Taylor, Justin. "An Interview with Steve Aylett." *Bookslut*. July 2006. 11 Jan. 2015.

"Tesseract." *The Oxford English Dictionary*. Seventh Edition. Oxford: Oxford University Press, 2013.

Speed, Originality and *Déjà vu* in *Bigot Hall*

Robert Kiely

> "With the speed we don't need
> in our vision we visit the closest
> city to total spirit, as awkward and
> as contingent as patriotism I eat
> the only book it lets me have."
> —Thomas Weber

We read the work of Steve Aylett with some level of bewilderment. His prose is uncompromisingly fast—its rapidity usually exceeds ratiocination, puts us on the alert, strains our nerves. Aylett's books are baroque in their density, speed, and finely crafted detail; they are overcrowded, they dazzle and distort and wait for us to catch up with their narrative world. I'd like to draw attention to the way in which Aylett's texts valorize their own speed, and offer some parallels and counterpoints drawn from certain innovative strains of contemporary literary practice. But before going any further, we must disambiguate speed into at least three categories: the first is speed of plot, the second speed of narrative delivery, the third speed of reading.

Typically Aylett's texts *negatively* broach the topic of speed by lambasting other novelists for being slow. *Atom (2000)* places John Updike in its crosshairs, describing a strange bomb from the remarkable Aylett armoury: "[T]he Syndication bomb hinged on a cheap but ingenious trick. Rather than actually stripping the subtext from the blast site it converted the wave range into a living Updike novel, the subtext containing information everyone already knew—the end result was a shallow reality in which every move was a statement of the obvious" (54). Updike simply *states the obvious*. All subtext becomes overt. But there is little mention of speed here. I will have to justify my thinking.

Kathryn Hume's analysis of "narrative speed" suggests that there are three means of speeding up a narrative, all of which work in conjunction: (a) multiplying the units (e.g., character, plot elements, etc. . . . in a word, content); (b) subtracting linking-material (because if you multiply elements but explain to the point of tedium their logical or sequential connection, the speed will, if anything, slow down); (c) departing from "consensus reality" and diving into "fantasmagoria," which is often a side-effect of point (b), i.e., things seem anomalous because they are not explained or connected logically (Hume 107, 111, 112). Updike's prose is clearly devoid of all of these points except possibly (a), but (a) without (b) results in a slower pace. Stating the obvious slows us down.

All of Hume's traits can be found in Aylett's prose. The content is there and plain to see; these are not conventionally difficult texts, they simply deliver their content in Aylett's sentences with an imposingly large bandwidth, and they come thick and fast, like a standup routine of one-liners delivered at the pace of Beckett's *Not I*. Think Groucho Marx running circles around you, the straight man. Rarely does Aylett clarify or paraphrase, and each sentence can feel so far removed from the last that they seem to be non-sequiturs. If Aylett's default speed is fast for the average reader, he is rightly proud of it. In private conversation, he told me: "My fiction delivers quickly. A novel's-worth can be delivered in a sentence, and then (if everything's working) I can move on to delivering another novel's-worth in the next sentence, and so on. A book should be worth it. The old cyberpunks used to assess each other on how much could be delivered with the fewest words (without resorting to academic code or language). I like compression."

Ernest Hemingway receives similar treatment to Updike in *Bigot Hall* (1995). As the subtitle states, *Bigot Hall* is a memoir of a gothic childhood with shades of the Addams family, the Flann O'Brien of *At Swim-Two-Birds* (1939) and *The Third Policeman* (1967), and Wilde's *The Picture of Dorian Gray* (1890). The book ends in a kind of blue-screen error message and a storm of self-conscious flux.

In chapter "SO WHAT," Adrienne claims that "*déjà vu* could be induced by arranging to have a condescending moron tell her something she already knew" (29). Again, stating the obvious, cliché, etc. But Adrienne seems to have such an excess of cognitive ability that experiences of this nature allow her to visit other "etheric bubbles" of "timespace" to compensate for any mansplaining administered to her in her own timestream. Ergo, in typically speedy-Aylett-logic, "[i]f several hundred *déjà vu* experiences were lined up in a row and experienced as a seamless stream it would be akin to a clusterbusting hallucination. Whole months of wasted time would be given back to us in a single hit" (29). If *déjà vu* here entails the repetition of something that has gone before, it is also the source of hallucinations that Adrienne and the nameless antihero get in compensation. Aylett zips past an implicit analogy, *déjà vu* and cliché all blurred from the reader's passenger window.

Hunting for further sources of *déjà vu*, the protagonist comes across a novel by Hemingway: "I happened upon a Hemingway volume in the reading room and found it was perfect. At no point was there the risk of being jarred back into realtime by a new idea. . . . Some of the ideas went beyond the obvious into a kind of homicidal vacuum. I saw a riotous play of lights on my skullwall as the crucifying boredom ricocheted me out of the timestream" (30). The prose waxes lyrical as Adrienne and the protagonist fly outside of the universe itself. "The universe opened like a flower, and we were gone. A billion miles below, the self-evident scrapped and sizzled like incinerating trash" (31). The nameless anti-hero and Adrienne have said "Goodbye to a world of re-run conversation and louts who swear blind that sand is yellow" (143). If Hemingway is boring, and the world is full of truisms, Aylett amply compensates. It is as if, like a reader, these characters can *skip the boring bits* of the *universe itself*. Adrienne and the nameless protagonist take this kind of speed-reading to be a mode of living. They skip over the bits of life in which she's telling him how she's been hurt before and she can't go through that again because it is commonplace dribble. Adrienne lives life as a speed-reader reads books. That is what Aylett asks of us.

In private correspondence, Aylett says that the "only Hemingway I could stick with was *A Moveable Feast*, which is a beautifully atmospheric thing." Although atmospheric, Hemingway's works are nonetheless wordy and repetitive; this might be positively phrased by emphasizing the lyrical refrains in his text.

I have hinted that speed might be valorized in a variety of ways. Does it beget the unexpected? Is it a pleasure in and of itself, a drug, an intensifier? Kathryn Hume points out that speed, like channel surfing, can produce irritation, bewilderment, or exhilaration (119). It is also a centrifuge, separating "hip" readers from "squares" (120). Hume also suggests that speed frequently correlates to literary high spirits and that the politics of speed seem radical, rebellious, and critical of rationality (Baetens and Hume 350). But there is a danger in identifying speed too neatly with pleasure, originality, or rebelliousness. Hume makes this mistake in her first consideration of the topic, claiming that "the politics of narrative speed seems to be radical or at any rate rebellious, with the authors being the rebels" (107). Yet if "the accumulation over time of authors and texts like these create familiarity, even comfort with the unstructured world," perhaps all is not so positive (122). The tediously painstaking and slow thinking that might be required to solve serious problems is something that fiction can help us to exercise, as in, say, Beckett's *Watt* (1953). Hume's sample texts all attack some form of authority, but in the collaboration with Baetens, the authors acknowledge that while "overall the politics of speed seem radical, rebellious, and critical of rationality" (350), no such neat identification of politics with form is possible:

> **artistic and narrative innovation and radicalism are not based on rapidity (as we tend to believe today) or on slowness (as we used to believe some decades ago), but rather oppose the accepted mainstream narrative speed, (a kind of 'average rhythm,' neither too fast nor too slow and having an accepted balance between fast**

and slow fragments). We suggest that various forms of counternarrative are characterized by noncanonical ways of manipulating rhythm that end up disturbing, either by slowing down or speeding up, the mainstream average rhythm. This average, of course, has no extrahistorical essence: it consists of a historically moving norm. (354)

Unlike the brief attacks on Updike and Hemingway, artistic and narrative innovation are not necessarily linked to rapidity, but simply oppose the accepted mainstream narrative speed: the *average rhythm* of prose that is neither too fast nor too slow. Of course, Aylett's work has to return to a slower pace at times. Kant's pigeon, feeling the resistance of the air, imagines that in a perfect vacuum flight would be easier. At times, *Bigot Hall* imagines that it can have speed in a pure form without the friction of repetition, when such resistance is what makes flight possible. The text must slow itself down sometimes, although it is so rare that it almost comes as a welcome relief, or becomes newly jarring: "They were looking horribly familiar - because they were the same ones as before. It was the same circus" (39). This is a relatively rare example of semi-paraphrase from one sentence to the next. Does this fast narrative encourage slow reading? Might the reader pause, reread, and unfold Aylett's tightly packed? In contrast to slow narrative, a speedy text might become a space for the reader to enter and make logical connections, something to unfurl and unpack. Poet and critic Keston Sutherland has suggested that speed-reading "is anti-philological. It is the avoidance, and perhaps even the refutation, of the 'hermeneutic circle' that philology sought to overcome through patient and repeated study of its texts" (40). Can Aylett's texts endure sustained scrutiny of the philological kind?

I'm not sure that the use of *déjà vu* in *Bigot Hall* stands up to such a reading, although other aspects of this work may reward such labor. When Aylett writes that Adrienne could have *déjà vu* "induced by arranging to have a condescending moron tell her something she already knew" (29), the *already-seen* moves quickly and seamlessly into the *already-known*, and the uncanny aspect of *déjà vu* is lost. Out of necessity, we are drawn along in this movement—the use of the terms seems slightly incongruous unless it is read at speed—if we stop here and think, the whole sentence falls onto its side like a bicycle—it has to *keep moving*. It is a matter of momentum. Aylett employs *déjà vu* for its immediate momentary impression in an idiosyncratic way, asking that the term be stretched and modified to fit the task at hand. Similarly, while the "etheric bubbles" are mysterious in origin, their flippancy demands that they be grasped quickly and dimly (not the *impertinently voluble*, but the flexible, limber, a lightness of touch, a nimble pliancy.) Trying to grasp these terms while moving at speed is difficult. When we slow down, the terms no longer seem fit for purpose.

Sutherland describes this as follows in his fourth thesis:

> **I mean by speed-reading a new and particular kind of hermeneutics, made for the first time valuable by some new work now being written in English. These texts demand to be read at speed. They self-falsify in the circle of hermeneutic patience:**

> **the more slowly and hesitantly they are read, the less of them is really there for the reader. The anticipated objection—that such texts cease to be interesting as soon as we scrutinize them attentively, and that they masquerade beneath the blur of their unfixed syntax as a kind of intelligence that can't actually be demonstrated through patient exposition - are both valid and obtuse.**

Aylett's prose is fast. It wants to be read fast, it wants its force to be felt in this quickness of blood, and it wants you to *get it*. And whereas Aylett is fast, he is anything but fragmented - his themes are immense and resurgent, from the failures of civilization (*Rebel at the End of Time* and *Novahead*), to originality and creativity and its opposition in the endless stupidity of the police (Eddie Gamete and Henry Blince). We need this speed, if only to counteract the regurgitated reposts and retweets and shares of mainstream publishing. I may be waxing into a mere advert here. But I am not regurgitating some horrendous avant-garde or modernist power stance. "Don't understand me too quickly - think about it" ("Specter's Way" 110).

It is not intrinsically bad to want fast humour, fast books, to want it *now*. Not in and of itself. The *Principles of Scientific Management* seeped into the world of literature long ago. Life is short and therefore rich and condensed is often for the best. Since life is short, though, try some slowness too. For all of his narrator's grumblings, they do not ask for their speed to be raised to the level of a standard. Until our average-narrative-pace-per-page increases, Aylett is likely to remain a strangely invigorating counterpoint to the status quo. Fast and steady wins the race every time.

Bigot Hall includes an *Inception*-like sequence in which the nameless antihero and Adrienne arrange to meet in a shared dream, then in dreams-within-dreams (125), each with increased temporal density. The antihero gets confused about what dream-level he inhabits and spends a lot of time damaging himself (126). When he awakens, Adrienne shows him how much time they have "wasted" in their dream-levels: "She showed me the bedside clock. We had been asleep nearly two minutes" (127). Aylett's works are the timesaving hallucinations that pack a month into a second. What we should do with the time he saves us is unclear.

Works Cited

"The Heart of the Original: Interview with Steve Aylett." *The Literary Platform*, 7 Aug. 2013. Web. 13 Sep. 2013.

Aylett, Steve. *Atom*. London: Phoenix, 2000.

Aylett, Steve. *Bigot Hall: A Gothic Childhood*. 1995. London: Indigo, 2000.

Aylett, Steve. *Smithereens*. Scar Garden Press, 2010.

———. "Specter's Way." *Smithereens*. London: Scar Garden Press, 2010.

Baetens, Jan, and Kathryn Hume. "Speed, Rhythm, Movement: A Dialogue on K. Hume's Article 'Narrative Speed." *Narrative* 14.3 (2006): 349-55.

Connor, Steven. "Slow Going." *The Yearbook of English Studies* 30 (2000): 153-65.

Coolidge, Clark. "Kerouac." 1995. Web. 13 Sep. 2013.

Dinh, Linh. "A Conversation with Brooks Johnson." *Harriet: A Poetry Blog*. 26 April 2012. Web. 15 Sep. 2013.

Goode, Chris. "An Introduction to Speed-Reading." *QUID* 15 (2005): 6-8.

Hemingway, Ernest. "A Good Café on the Place St-Michel." *A Moveable Feast*. 1964. London: Arrow, 2004.

———. *A Moveable Feast*. 1964. London: Arrow, 2004.

Hume, Kathryn. "Narrative Speed in Contemporary Fiction." *Narrative* 13.2 (2005): 105-24.

Sutherland, Keston. "Four Theses on Speed (from an Ongoing Series)." *QUID* 12 (2004), 38-41.

Weber, Tomas, "Auscultation." *An Official Word from Me out of Uniform*. Tokyo: Tipped Press, 2012.

Review of the Velocity Gospel

Michael Moorcock

The most influential absurdist to emerge from 1950s science fiction was Robert Sheckley. Books such as *Mindswap* and *Dimension of Miracles* furnished Douglas Adams with an entire cabinet of borrowed curiosities.

Sheckley remains an inspiration for almost every funny SF and fantasy author writing today, but he didn't invent humorous SF. It has a long tradition, including Kurt Vonnegut's *Sirens of Titan* (1959), Harry Harrison's *Bill, The Galactic Hero* (1966), Charles Platt's *Garbage World* (1967) and the great John Sladek's *The Muller-Fokker Effect* (1970). Then there is Maurice Richardson's classic *Exploits of Engelbrecht* (1950), recently republished by Savoy, which is also a riot of the surreal and the absurd.

Lately, as desperately needed antidotes to nerd-friendly space fiction and inklingoid fantasy, writers such as David Britton, Rhys Hughes, Jeff VanderMeer and Tim Etchells have set their fiction in invented worlds satirically parallel to our own, inhabited by eccentric characters enthusiastically embracing irrationality and paradox.

One of the best of these new absurdists is Steve Aylett. His early mysteries were like Hammett on bad acid, in which fast-talking detectives solved metaphysical crimes and sported weapons firing philosophical concepts rather than bullets. *The Crime*

Studio (1994), *Bigot Hall* (1995) and S*laughtermatic* (1997) were set in the unlikely world of Beerlight. Last year he published the wonderful *Shamanspace* (2001), in which God was found to exist, causing various parties to seek vengeance against him.

Only an Alligator (2001) was the first in a new fantasy trilogy featuring the city of Accomplice, whose map includes the Church of Automata, the Ultimatum Restaurant and the Juice Museum. In this novel Barny Juno, who possesses a useful affinity for large animals, gets up the noses of some serious demons, saving himself with the help of his friends Edgy and Gaffer and an amiable shaman called Beltane Carom. The demons and their chief, Sweeney, are as cheerfully demented as the citizens of Accomplice, whose corrupt and greedy mayor is the only organ of government.

The Velocity Gospel (2002) is the even funnier sequel. Here Sweeney, though thoroughly thwarted by Barny, is still determined to have satisfaction, and sends his emissary Skittermite aloft to exact it. "Because those bastards are completely covered in skin they think they can deny their insides… The sheer architectural extravagance of demonic biology was mostly open to inspection, infernodyne veins and pulsing bile yolk fully visible through wide-flung ribs."

Meanwhile, the unwholesome Gaffer lusts after a mechanical clock and gets sucked into Accomplice's latest radical cult, The Friends of Cyril, originally invented as a public diversion by the mayor but now gathering its own reality. Their creed is contained in the Velocity Gospel, and their slogans appear all over the city: TRY OUR LAYERED MOODS and LET ROAD MURDERS YO YO. Skittermite makes unsuccessful attempts on Barny's vitals, only to be thwarted by his lions and chimps. Barny seeks shamanic advice for his love life (Chloe Lowe or Magenta Blaze?) and receives wisdom which satisfies him but confuses us. You can't afford to skip through Aylett's idiosyncratic eloquence, and there's no easy way of further summarizing the story without reducing it to something else. So much depends on tone and inference. The plot races as fast as it thickens, and reaches its existentialist resolution as Barny shacks up with Chloe. "I love it here" are his final words. We are promised more fun ahead.

Reminiscent of Ronald Firbank's *Concerning Eccentricities of Cardinal Pirelli* (1926) or *Sorrow in Sunlight* (1924), Aylett's language is often the substance, the narrative. You are lost unless you accept the logic of his characters, the sardonic rhythms of his prose. And as with Firbank, you tend to begin an Aylett feeling that you've been dropped into the annual party at the loony bin, but after a few pages his weirdly angled vision takes you over.

By the end of the book it all seems perfectly logical, while the world around you is definitely askew. This is his genius—if you give him your time, he'll return you solid value, an enjoyable rollercoaster ride. But you'll never be entirely sure of what you've heard or where you've been.

The Aylett Effect

Jim Matthews

"In a sort of epilogue, the boy, now a sorcerer, opens a stream and points at its inner structure, cages and cages receding into infinity."[1]

If that line from Aylett's *Lint* leaves you cold, you might be best skipping the rest of this piece. If it startles you and sets your brain fizzling at some level, well, here I want to try to look at that effect. What it is about Aylett's writing that's so arresting and disturbing on first contact, before the analytical brain kicks in and the (arguably) submerged meanings rise to the surface. What the subsequent effect is and why it's so valuable.

It's been said of Rimbaud, Pynchon and several others that a certain *state of mind* is induced by reading them. For me the same's true of some Surrealist literature (the good stuff as opposed to the piles of dreck) and, with bewildering frequency, of Aylett's work too. I don't personally read Rimbaud for his underlying message, because frankly I find it's rarely worth having. I certainly wouldn't say that of Aylett, but it's that mind-state I want to focus on. He considers his satire operates like a bomb planted in the mind and I want to suggest that a comparable effect comes as much from *how* he says things as any

---

[1] It's considered bad practice to begin with a quote - and that's good enough for me...

underlying messages. For this I've drawn most heavily on *Novahead* - a book about a boy with a bomb actually in his mind – because I think the aspects I want to point up are concentrated there as strongly as anywhere.

Reading a writer as eclectic as Aylett inevitably calls previous writers and writing traditions to mind. Perhaps some of the comparisons made here will seem trite or glib but I think the general exploration's worthwhile, if only to get some argument going in the area. Plenty's been said already about the excess of potential meaning in individual sentences, and I believe the magic doesn't consist wholly in that - though it may well be enhanced *by* it.

I'm going to start with the Surreal and Absurd. Some people probably approach a Surrealist line such as "the exquisite cadaver will drink the new wine," as a puzzle to be solved; and it certainly encourages it. At first the striking imagery is baffling, but a key is found when we read it in a liturgical context – the cadaver is that of Christ (exquisite = divine), and the wine represents the infusion of his blood during communion; with its properties of spiritual rejuvenation. As such the line refers to the resurrection, the second coming and the triumph of life over death. The puzzle's been decoded then, but was that the main purpose? Is the satisfaction of solving the primary benefit to be had, and is the message *itself* – a pretty bog-standard Christian tenet – the real power here?

Surrealist and Absurdist literature can even, arguably, *diminish* in power when interpretation is nailed down. In Ionesco's *The Lesson*, the murderous professor dons a swastika armband at the end of the play, and it's been said that this act of grounding the work in a specific historical/political context has a deflating effect. An otherwise completely symbolical work gets fixed in parameters of time and locality, and something of the resonance is lost.

It can of course go the other way, and reader subjectivity plays a big part. With the Surrealist line: "the man cut in half by the window," my own reaction to attaining some of its possible significances is of a similar reduction of effect: The window's divided frames appear to bisect the figure of the man seen in it, or the man is the author who's discovered the Surrealist phenomenon of "the marvellous" and has glimpsed his own interiority, Damien-Hirst-cow style. However no interpretation takes primacy, and so its capacity to resonate isn't totally stilled.

What I want to argue is that the *effect* here doesn't *come* from meaning as much as from form; especially in Surrealism where a concerted, deliberate distance is said to be created by the artist between the two.

A counter argument to the above is that I'm making a false division here, between expression and meaning; between form and message. Of course there's no distinct line, but deriving literal meaning from very abstract writing ultimately involves cashing it out in rational terms; as has been done above. When Aylett writes "the city was creaking with corners," one possible interpretation is that the narrator feels increasingly trapped at every turn: cornered on all sides. Or, we might infer some comment on the geometrical layout of this city run awry – its psychogeographical effects of constriction and paranoia, even – which hark back to the earlier line, "Beerlight was like most cities in that fear was the master builder." *Or*, abstracting further, a comment on the nature of Beerlight society and the experience of living there among its denizens and leaders. But just *saying* it like that - while also narrowing the scope for interpretation and projection - strips it of its immediate, oneiric power.

In *The Rise of Surrealism*, Willard Bohn (paraphrasing Andre Breton's manifesto for Surrealism) states:

> **Every Surrealist image must have an analogical component [but] to be effective the analogy must remain undetected on the surface...must trigger a response at a deeper level. This explains the reader/viewer's involuntary shudder on encountering one of the more powerful images**.

Breton himself said "beauty demands to be enjoyed usually before being understood and...tolerates elucidation only *a posteriori* and as though outside itself." Bohn sums up this second point: "The spectator's task is first to perceive the literal image and register its emotional impact. To the extent that it conforms to the definition in the manifesto it will be received with astonishment."

Aylett insists that this distancing of meaning from expression – in the manner set down above as actually *essential* to surrealist writing - isn't his intention. And he should know. But I don't think that really matters in the quest to explore effect. My point is not that meaning is less important, but that its clarification (often but not always) *trails behind*, is delayed, and so can't account for that up-front impact.

Bohn's remarks, however, suggest that Surrealist meanings, though forcibly distanced, register on the reader at the same time, somehow, but at a deeper level. Well, that idea calls into play all kinds of questions on the nature of mind, the unconscious, and so on; which fall outside the scope of this essay. So when I talk about the meaning being grasped I mean its conscious, literal clarification. And in *that* sense I think it's safe to talk about delay and distance in Aylett.

Breton said that words have their own emotional life which permits them to respond to each other according to secret affinities. The Surrealists used cut-ups and other techniques to deliberately generate unconventional associations between words and ideas. Aylett himself says:

Sometimes there'll be two words which have never been put next to each other before because they "belong" in different environments & so most people will never hold them at the same time - to me these will magnetise together because they obviously have something to say together.

In Aylett's worlds, dead waterfronts exude "fish nostalgia," an English country squire pronounces his own face a "dismal jamboree" (made of pasta, for that matter), planets are brittle and the sky itches. Eisenhower is deemed a "florid psychopath." There are quantum punchlines, quantum strumpets, and magotty stories. Crackpot Bonifaces, gun karma, a flesh stylus. Bantamweight roses. Train epiphany[2]. Defects in the grain of the sky. The corner-spindle of a spider.

There's tons and tons of this. An effervescence of perturbing incongruities. Words banged together to produce sparks.

---

[2] I hear that one tooting and whistling dark revelations in steam.

A familiar idea in literary (and other) theory is that an artist can convey significances he doesn't consciously intend but which legitimately inhere in the forms he's chosen; dredged up from the unconscious, swimming with influences from the common ocean. This invites and validates projection on the reader's part.

Although Aylett says, when asked, that he always knows *at some level* what he means, he goes on to describe the synaesthetic, sculptural form in which books arrive *en bloc* in his mind and to expound:

I tend to think in shapes and colours rather than words so at its most abstract it may come down to whether the shape is viable/coherent (whether it operates). When a book arrives all the meaning is implicit in the shape/image.

It would be obtuse of me to speculate on *where he gets it from*. I hope it's forgivable, however, to say the quote above at least subjects the notion of 'meaning' to heavy qualification. A bone-dry academic might want to gnaw a bit on the question of whether Aylett always intends what he writes to be interpreted in specific ways, and whether he lays sufficient ground for it.

Returning to the quote I started with then, it can mean various things or nothing[3], depending on the reader, but I suggest that getting them doesn't account for the experience or even necessarily enhance it. That image can only strike the reader the way it does in the

---

[3] Perhaps it relates to the more decipherable line (from *And Your Point is?*): 'A clock is a cage placed in a flowing stream; holding nothing, stopping nothing, not even for a minute.'

form it's presented in. There's an intuitive and emotive *totality* that surmounts the restrictions of discursive language in a way reminiscent of Beckett. Beckett's language is also complex, many-layered and reveals much hidden information under scrutiny, but an awareness of the more obscured references in *Krapp's Last Tape* isn't essential to obtaining that singular totality, the sense of a man's whole life transmitted through clips of a tape recording. That profound and intense experience consists in its wholeness and its ability to affect us all at once, as an unalloyed and undivided phenomenon; not dissected and laid out piecemeal.

Another writer worth bringing in at this point is Kafka. Aylett's writing frequently exhibits a vibrant relationship with his, at multiple levels, and with regard to what I've said so far it's worth digging into.

The philosophers Deleuze and Guattari see Kafka's books as machines – machines geared to producing profound effects in the reader. They identify "machinic assemblages…of human cogs and wheels" in his stories: the duos and trios of power-relations (Oedipal and others) that can at once resonate with political, familial, religious and other overtones without ever being finally pinned down: "Neither allegory, nor metaphor, nor theology will sum up a work which has explored them all without letting itself be taken over by a single one." Excess of meaning reverberates but it is *effect*, not metaphorical interpretation, that is paramount, they argue. Words become liberated from their role as signifiers in order to attain the highest *intensification*. "Language stops being referential in order to move towards its extremities or limits."

In their analysis, Kafka's use of language is intended to effect a "schizo-escape" by shedding traditional signification. No word, or image, ultimately refers or points to anything outside of itself. Liberated from their traditional role, they become "asignifying" and the language of sense, where words are rooted in meaning, is traversed by a "line of escape." As such, words have all the significance, in the traditional sense, of Gregor Samsa's progressively incomprehensible gibbers and twitters, and all the power to startle, horrify or affect the emotive, imaginative or instinctive plane.

Therefore the term 'machine' is used in a *concrete*, not a metaphorical, sense. A superabundance of possible meaning is there, but the machines are intended to be practised for their effects. Should any one interpretation claim primacy – should the work be finally pinned down – the chief power would be lost, the machine brought to rest and rendered defunct. It's not the multiplicity of possible meanings that endows the work with its power, but that element does enable its continuation.

In Deleuze and Guattari's take, the word is no longer a signifier but a thing in itself. It's an idea that shoots off in diverse theoretical directions, but I'll step quickly and try to avoid embarrassing myself.

The German philosopher Ernst Cassirer called this intensive concentration of words *hypostatisation* - using words in a way that their evocative power is so strong it becomes a presence in the room, alters your mind state there and then, not as a result of interpreting and considering a rational idea. He identified two separate functioning types of language: Rational, discursive language, which is systemic and referential - suited to theoretical thinking and logic, which features strict analogy and metaphor (fully decodable) - and purely *symbolical* language, which he considers the primordial manner of language-formation. This second of the "twinned streams of language" is pre-logical, and informs things like myth. There's a lot of crap talked about myth and I should be careful here, but, very basically, for those societies in which it played an active role, this hypostatisation, this notion of actual presence and effectiveness, inhered in words to the extent that the word *was* the thing it called to mind.[4]

Not, of course, that either Aylett or Kafka are doing that, or are writing anything like myths in the original sense: the ancient myths were actually believed and informed the running of society. But I think they also drew some of their force, again, from the induction of a mind-state in the listener or reader; a power that inhered in the way words and ideas were stacked up; rooted in that 'substratum of truth' and striking at the core. Perhaps another observation of Aylett's helps to nail this down a bit more concretely:

> **Terence McKenna talked about 'linguistic objects' or images which embody an idea or bundle of information [and which] don't need unpacking - the image/object is the meaning. At a very low-grade level of this, to describe someone as 'a wishbone in a coat' tells us a lot about that person/figure without us understanding why. The best poetry works that way & better, not needing any analysis.**

---

[4] And not in a postmodernist sense of taking the label for the object. More in the way of invoking the dead by speaking their names, for example.

In the work of a (precious) few other writers, we find moments of comparable effect. Aylett's is full of them.

To go any further down this road of myth and symbol takes us close to the Freudian view; something I'd rather avoid and which doesn't interest him either. In the most unintellectual sense, then, I mean that there's a vital current, like a crackling electric bolt, running through various world myths, Rimbaud, the Surrealists, Kafka, (probably others) and Aylett.

For sparing you the fun of Freud, I hope I'll be tolerated - having brought up this theme of altered mind-states - for introducing another chestnut. A soundbite from *The Scotsman,* typical of some of the comment Aylett attracts from time to time, reads: "If Aylett isn't on drugs, then his mind must be either fantastically psychedelic or scarily unhinged."

Another, from *Strange Horizons*: "British writer Steve Aylett has been plying his narcotics-fuelled SF satire for nearly a decade now..."

There it is - the old *hallucinatory prose* cliché, wheeled out to the detriment of untold artists, Lewis Carrol *et al*, as though to suggest that chemicals themselves can account for the output of a vibrant, fertile imagination and singular talent.

Yet I can see why in this case, because I've sat in dirty squat parties on ketamine and mushrooms, watching the air contort at the periphery and all the planes on someone's face become cornered and angular, as words open up on hidden sides and trains of innocent conversation suddenly acquire a disconcerting sense of undertow. And reading Aylett sometimes carries a genuine whiff of such moments at the intuitive level. Whether he actually *does* drugs is immaterial; his prose sometimes *works* like a drug, I'm saying. Like some of Rimbaud's poems do. And they really *do*.

Perhaps fortunately, when you start talking like that you've probably gone as far as theory can take you.

Returning to the link between writing and machinery designed for drastic effect, this is made explicit in Kafka's *In the Penal Colony*. The condemned man is supposed to experience a moment of spiritual epiphany upon deciphering the message mechanically inscribed on his flesh with metal needles. However, since he doesn't speak French (the language in which the officer explains this process to the traveller invited to witness the slow execution), the tortuous method of communication and the promise of redemption may be false. Since the soldier guarding the prisoner also doesn't speak French, however, and we're told nothing about the region, the point remains ambiguous. The single image of the machine reverberates in the mind and rattles out its concentrated cartridge of meaning upon the nature of language, power, corruption, punitive systems, art and crime, truth, religion and morality.

The comparison of writing to effect-geared machinery also surfaces in *Novahead. Haruspex Virus*, a pseudo-sacred text by venerated Beerlight author Eddie Gamete, works "like a device built for stress-testing prejudice, and because such beliefs will buckle under an instant's examination, the remaining excess torque [tends] to rip the reader open". Another book by the same author "lays down the architecture of a linear accelerator in the reader's mind. This device was activated by a single concept at the end of the text." Devices are activated, levers thrown, effects produced.[5]

---

[5] A 3:AM reviewer writes (of the *Accomplice* series): "It's a groaning

Other memorable machines and devices in Beerlight include a cloaking device for a car which operates by projecting whatever the onlooker doesn't want to acknowledge; capitalising on the human tendency to form psychological blindspots, even to our own detriment and danger. The *ibeam* – which presumably also works by retinal projection – is used to clarify a tricky premise by depicting an exploded diagram of the argument; perhaps similar to the way Aylett himself claims to see ideas. There are Kafkacell guns and eschaton rifles. Speculative fiction commonly features outlandish devices, but they rarely come as portmanteau images loaded with philosophical significance.

Aylett is known for his condensed, compressed style and at times the innovations crammed into his novels try the form beyond its limits; not subverting it so much as subordinating it to get his ideas across. "It's a fact that (in my own writing) I'm not primarily interested in story telling but ideas, gags and images," he explains. *Novahead* appropriates the *detective-with-one-last-case* flat-pack as a housing for poetic, philosophical and satirical fun and games which at times poke out through its windows and make holes in the roof. He frequently speaks of "getting rid of an idea" (his phrasing) in a few words which another author would devote a whole book to, and of having had his time wasted by books in which one or two original ideas are spun out over hundreds of pages. This attitude is key to approaching pretty much any of his work.

Take a subject like the nature of interrogation, as practiced and documented in the war on terror and

---

perpetual motion machine, decked out as a funfair attraction."

various repressive regimes from history. Researching accounts from Guantanamo Bay and Stasi prisoners, etc, an author might bring out the irrational and retrograde side to procuring intelligence through torture in successive novel scenes, closing in with a master's steady hand on that impalpable psychological hinterland between the questioner and the questioned – in which each must pull words from the air, consciously or unconsciously taking the cue from the other. As Aylett puts it:

An interrogation is not just a form of emotional feasting, it's really a form of divination. Its arcane conditions are supposed to conjure information that none of those taking part actually know. A setup designed to expect deception will tend to generate it, bending information into 'true' by forced surmise. Everyone comes out ahead.

Aylett handles such a situation by stating it – stripped down to the bare bones, the fewer words the better. Having nailed it with a poetic image, a 'gag' or other intensely memorable device, he moves on to something else. In that regard his approach is *extensive*, rather than *intensive*. We get a book full of such stuff - not necessarily that deeply or tightly interconnected, except on the level of surface story; which, as noted, is not of paramount concern.

There are pros and cons to this extensive style. Other books give us a sense, through the rigorous exploration and development of a theme, that something quite like *proof* is being established. Things are demonstrated, substantiated; like a meticulously constructed legal case. Maybe Aylett doesn't particularly expect you to believe him or doesn't really care, but either way he wastes little time on persuasions and justifications. There are new ideas up ahead to get down.

Given this and other aspects discussed, we might wonder why he chooses the novel form at all. One might even posit that he *doesn't,* entirely; his books are thoroughly hybrid things, meta-creatures with little regard for partition.

Of course there's a long tradition of novels of which that might be said; from Sterne through Calvino and others. But they're subverting and ironising the form, as an intellectual project in itself. I don't get the sense that Aylett's doing that. There may be some anticipation of his position in the work of Flann O'Brien – whose finest book, rejected in his own lifetime, also anticipated Calvino by several decades. *The Third Policeman* plays constant, elaborate games with reality and with various scientific, philosophical, mythical and other ways of observing and couching human experience; rather than just with written styles and traditions – to the extent that the reader is forced to repeatedly question the narrative territory. Aylett's decision to write within genre perhaps doubly sets the seal on his own literary obscurity.

Aylett's a cold fish; unconcerned to engage reader sympathy through the established means considered sacrosanct in the *how-to-write-a-novel-right* industry. Characters are as fleshed-out as they need to be for purpose. They display a stark deficit of warmth, emotional depth or complexity, and experience few moments of intimacy and vulnerability[6] that even

46

writers like Iain Banks - once considered dangerous - make sure to honour. They aren't, particularly, people.

There's intellectual depth, certainly, but not in the way it's more usually worked into novels. The arguments in *Novahead* aren't developed gradually, demonstrated and explored through action and situations, sneaked up on the reader through changing relationships and slow-dawning realizations of characters. They're stated outright. In more or less oblique or poetic ways, but pretty flatly nonetheless. The philosophy is mouthed so directly that at times the 1-D characters recede to the thickness of those in a school textbook - a torso, limbs and head fronting a linguistic or mathematical structure. You could have just slipped into a tract like Plato's *Republic*; except that the arguments are also far less drawn-out. Efficiency is shackled to economy, and ruthless he is about it. So, no smooth rides, no easing into the world of a new book like a warm room full of old, worn-in novel-furniture. Other novelists take great care to settle you in. Aylett doesn't just not do that, he seems to show a certain disdain. Sustaining an illusory "novel" world in the traditional sense is way down his list, and you can often feel you're no longer *in one*. Just as characters periodically attain the thickness of the paper they're on, the element of story *itself* is sometimes stretched as thin as that of the *Republic*; and anyone who reads that for its narrative qualities needs to get out more.

---

[6] Not that there aren't *any*. There's a certain valedictory note to Atom's reflections in *Novahead*, which confers a strange serenity against the backdrop of cynicism and extravagance. And in *Shamanspace* a flitting moment near the end perhaps recalls Rutger Hauer's tears-in-rain soliloquy, and, like it, is the more emotionally stark for its rarity.

This inevitably invites the response, *who cares* what label you put on it – 'novel' or whatever?

Right enough, but I want to note just how thoroughly unsettling this can be. Because how can you stay comfortably on course, settle in and glide along with your feet up, half awake, on the rails of a story whose barflies shoot the shit like they're solving a cryptic crossword - and a Mexican standoff between cops and robbers sounds like an avant-garde poetry recital? Where the jaded gumshoe narrator ventures desultory aperçus on the deteriorating aura of his assailant. You fall out of the novel world into something resembling a surreal political tract, a course textbook for some other dimension; or, conversely, into a plane of existence where people think and talk this way and these things make sense. The hero's car is powered by a friction caused by infinitesimal differences in time-zones from nose to bumper. A road battle is pronounced a "curate's egg" by the survivors. You're forced to constantly reassess your surroundings.

In the moments Aylett somehow strings together, in *Novahead* and *Shamanspace*, the *reader* is Joseph K. Moving through an illogical terrain, trying to gather clues as to what makes this place tick, to find the frequency which everyone but he is implicitly tuned into, that informs everything like an alien language. You have to look at things afresh and at times, that effect doesn't stop when you put the book down.

I've lent his books to people who returned them, saying they couldn't get into them, and he's not an easy read - forever jarring the reader out of one environment into another. It took me a few tries to get plugged in to *Accomplice*. But when he pulls things like that, it can force an abrupt gap in your internal schema; just for a short while you see things a little differently, start making connections of your own. It acts in a viral way and it's instinctive, provoking a creative response. The more cogent reviews seem to evidence this provocation.

D. Harlan Wilson writes: "every sentence in [*Novahead*] - in some cases, every word - is an intricate mountain god."

And Bill Ectric writes (of *Lint*):

It's like opening a pop-up book to see gemstones and charms strung together on bracelet chains, rising to display the black noir onyx, the blood-red ruby, the diamond center of the mind, the flaming gold-leaf giraffe trinket of surrealism.

More conventional reviews, particularly those that focus on plot (*Atom is a private eye in a futuristic world, who…*) seem to miss the point. The two people quoted above are fiction authors in their own right, which accounts for the intensely imagistic phrasing, but I get a sense that that take is ignited at the source level by the Aylett effect. They aren't the only ones to write like this about him, and I've resisted the impulse to do so myself because this is an effort to get away from abstract observation towards something more analytically cold (however wrong-headed that might be). I could be wrong about all this; I only know that after reading some, my brain starts working that way, more so than at other times. It's like being suddenly reminded of a part of your mind that's ignored.

Not everyone will get it, of course, and considering his frustratingly marginal position in the literary world, perhaps he's more of a writer's writer - providing a shot in the arm for those who write in a more thinned-down and easily digestible style (which is almost everyone).

I'll invite and deserve a lot of flak if I don't at least briefly state that Aylett's work goes a lot deeper than just first effects, and often no distinction can be made. The satirical element of his work is strung throughout like hi-tensile electric fence-wire and is, for him, paramount. He says:

> **People have lost touch with what real satire is - they confuse it with cheap sarcasm - but the real thing works like a bomb which gets deep into your head before exploding. As with a vampire you actually invite it in unawares and then all hell breaks loose when it reveals itself. Satire disguises itself as something you agree with, uses your own innards against you. Genesis P. Orridge talks about metabolic music, whereby a certain combination of notes, maybe stumbled on by accident, can cause an explosive ascension in the listener, transforming from the cellular level upwards. I'd like to do something like that by a combination of words. Make the reader's head explode. But in a nice way.**

Aylett situates his own satire as in direct line from Voltaire; another author who doesn't suffer character or plot development to hold up his campaign (in *Candide*) against the moronic and dangerous wisdom of his time - stressing and stretching Leibniz' best-of-all-possible-worlds philosophy till the holes gape and the reader feels it, in the manner of Gamete's *Haruspex Virus*.

Until his ludicrously miserable odyssey forces him to think critically, Candide faithfully espouses Prof. Pangloss' Leibnizian doctrine – which the latter routinely 'proves' by turning the world on its head. As such, noses are fashioned (perfectly) by the creator to support glasses, the importation of syphilis is a mere downside to the venture that brought chocolate and a particular food-dye to Europe, and the rape and butchery of people minding their own business in one village is made up for by the same thing happening in another village just over the border. With elegant simplicity, disease, religious cant and murder overlap and analogise each other, and are all inextricably entwined with the crowning concept of "sufficient reason."

Pangloss' (perennial, damnable) optimism on "development" runs like this:

> **It is also to be observed, that, even to the present time, in this continent of ours, this malady, like our religious controversies, is peculiar to ourselves. The Turks, the Indians, the Persians, the Chinese, the Siamese, and the Japanese are entirely unacquainted with it; but there is sufficient reason for them to know it in a few centuries.**

Aylett revels in surgically excising this kind of skewed thinking, which looks like paradox but is actually just idiotic sophistry of the most lethal mix. In *The Crime Studio*, while repeatedly roping crime and art/fashion together in a manner that simmers over

51

with implications, Aylett cuts through the sophistry that justifies the punitive system with a sliver of exposition on the Beerlight penitentiary, where "it was the fashion to punish crooks severely so as to encourage their assimilation back into the underworld - a process known as 'recrimination.'" Simultaneously, this manages to lampoon smug liberal ideology as well. As always, there's a lot going on.

I want to end by trying to convey something of what reading Aylett means to me personally. On the run up to the first Gulf War, as *our boys* were massed on the Kuwaiti border, there was a brief moment (I wonder if anyone else remembers it now?) where we supposedly hovered on the brink of a climb-down; war might be averted after all. A British Tory politician voiced the view that it would be regrettable, having got the troops all prepared to *go in,* to let them down at this stage. I was 16 and I remember people around me - parents, teachers, peers - pick up that idea and pass it on, along with all the other sumptuous prating and grandstanding we were vigorously echoing. I got a feeling, in a way I couldn't myself properly articulate, that active, independent thought had died a public death at a time of international crisis. Society was sick and mad with a kind of omni-banality and the course of bloodshed was being kept on the table - with our complacent approval - for the most vapid of non-arguments.

That feeling, needless to say, has been replicated innumerable times since.

Aylett wasn't around then but for what my opinion's worth, he doesn't just encourage active thought, he *forces* it; forging new links between words and ideas, busting stale and received ones apart. Art's supposed to do that anyway, but it usually works in a much more diluted way if at all. It's Aylett's concentrated intensity that makes his writing stand apart. After an attentive reading of *Lint* or *Novahead* you might come through just a little bit changed.

I wouldn't stretch comparisons with Blake too far, but the concepts of 'mental fight' and of trusting in one's own interiority, of never losing sight of one's capacity for individual vision, are as alive and vital to Aylett as to Blake– and his linguistic innovations and the effects wrought thereby are as much at the service of that as are his disparate observations on power, society and so on, and his acid-satire. Ionesco said, "to renew the language is to renew the conception, the vision of the world." This is the true direction of force, underlying his splintering and plasticising of words, his almost violent shake-up of stale language and concepts.

It's been mooted in various reviews and write-ups that much of the *Lint* material is thinly-veiled *Aylett-on-Aylett*, if only as he would like to be, what he is aiming for:

> **…his sentences have substances stored in their roots that will be released only after time…Each point is the head of a thread, a retrievable plumb-line of information …**
> **More than one reader has witnessed green-gold flukes opening in the page before clenching their eyes and looking again at innocent print.**

Should we take Aylett at his own valuation (if that's what this is) here? My own reaction to his prose, while strong, still falls short of such a dazzling, dizzying synaesthetic experience. Maybe his next book will have me *actually* seeing stars.

Can the Aylett effect really "ambush the reader into magnanimity"? Is it really possible that a few people might actually end up being a bit nicer to one another, if their eyes are slightly more opened? If this, again, is mere ambition, it's still nobler than what drives most writers.

Aylett has no illusions about changing anything by reflecting truths - social or other - in satire. He knows "the mirror holds no fear for those without shame." And perhaps this, too, affirms my suggestion that meaning trails behind. Because what he *can* do is become "true north for clear-eyed resenters" - i.e. a clear beacon for those awake and alive enough to despise cliché and re-run in fiction and, more dangerously, fact. To need more.

The last few quotes, from *And Your Point Is*, are perhaps the clearest statement of the (suitably humble) "grand purpose" implicit throughout his fiction. This finally becomes *explicit* in his first non-fiction work, where I'd say style and message become more closely fused than anywhere else. *Heart of the Original* exhorts readers to *use* their "resentment" at a world kept stale, to rediscover the fertile infinite that is everyone's birthright, in order to create fresh, astounding work of their own - or, if not, then just to live more vitally in the here and now. "You can sit on a bus and do it."

Cult status notwithstanding, however, there's no call for a church of Aylett: "After doing the cure, you're on your own." Those electrified by his writing needn't hang around in mawkish fandom. "Hero worship is like misheard lyrics – they are never as good as you thought." Take what it gives you and run with it.

The Wonderful and Frightening Worlds of Mark E. Smith and Steve Aylett

Spencer Pate

"The difference between you and us is that we have brains."
—"Intro" [*Totale's Turns*] by The Fall

An author as original as Steve Aylett compels us to territorialize his imagination, to annex it to what we already know and understand. When the laziest reviewers of *Lint* (2005) noticed the novel's superficial parallels and allusions to the life of Philip K. Dick, they automatically assumed it was intended as a *roman à clef* and proceeded to criticize it on this basis . . . notwithstanding Aylett's assertions to the contrary in several interviews. (To be fair, the book may have been marketed misleadingly in this regard.) While Jeff Lint was not intended to be a thinly-disguised Philip K. Dick, Aylett may have had other models and analogues in mind—namely Mark E. Smith (or, as fans call him, MES), the lead singer, lyricist, and sole constant member of that British post-punk institution The Fall. I certainly do not mean to suggest that *Lint* was extrapolated from MES's colorful life, only to assert that his contrarian persona and distinctive approach to cultural criticisms have strongly informed the satirical work of Steve Aylett and, by extension, Jeff Lint. My intention is not to find and catalogue every instance in Aylett's fiction where he alludes to The Fall (although, as an avowed fan, Aylett places many such references throughout his *oeuvre*). Rather, I want to delineate and compare the satirical currents in MES and Aylett's idiosyncratic bodies of work.

For readers unfamiliar with The Fall's music, let me recommend their near-perfect run of albums, extended plays, singles, live recordings, and Peel Sessions from 1977 to 1985, which constitutes one of the most astonishing sequences in the history of rock music. I also loved Dave Simpson's fascinating and hilarious book *The Fallen* in which he tracks down and interviews nearly every ex-member of The Fall. (MES, you see, is infamously eccentric and difficult to work with; he has hired, fired, psychologically tested, and physically fought countless members throughout the band's 35-year history.)

My first encounter with the music of The Fall was remarkably similar to the first time I read Aylett's fiction. I felt a deep rapport with both artists, intellectually and emotionally. I suspect this is because all of our positive experiences with cult fiction or cult music can be explained *structurally* (and Aylett and MES are nothing if not cult figures; they tend to inspire obsessive devotion among their most ardent fans). By its very nature, a cult work of art must reject the ideal of broad accessibility and strike a precise balance between inclusion and exclusion, alienating what it perceives to be the mainstream yet seeming inclusive, special, and above all *truthful* to those who feel always-already alienated from mass culture. It must make one feel *smart*. Aylett's *Lint*, for example, is the kind of book a cult fan cherishes to the extent that he or she buys multiple copies to give away to friends in hopes of initiating them into the cult, as it were.

On the level of content, cult fiction and music often short-circuits lowbrow and highbrow culture in order to launch an assault on the totality of society. Formally, it might be raw, abrasive, and messy . . . much like The Fall's noisy, lo-fi music, which stylistically draws upon punk, rockabilly and krautrock; foregrounds a heavy, repetitive rhythm section; and features MES's absolutely inimitable vocal delivery. This musical firewall is in turn mirrored by MES's cantankerous-but-endearing persona, general misanthropy, and cryptic, intelligent, scathingly witty lyrics. Aylett's work shares this quality of being highly epigrammatic.

At its cynical worst, a cult work of art merely flatters and congratulates the ostensibly superior intelligence of its audience without tendering a positive vision in opposition to its critical targets. At its best— as with Aylett or The Fall—the work of art will perform a negation of the negation, uniting a ruthless, radical critique of existing society with the postulation of alternative possibilities. In this process, it may also create a real sense of community among its audience. It's not a coincidence that so many popular works of cult fiction are satirical in nature. Essentially satire isn't a genre unto itself, but rather an artistic tool of the oppressed and alienated. Proper satire is incompossible with power; like all true comedy, it does not forgive.

In interviews, Aylett invariably rejects genre labels and allegiances, preferring instead to identify himself as a satirist. Rightly so—his work contains all the hallmarks of classic satire. I will discuss these satirical elements in turn, tracing some possible lines of descent from MES's songs to Aylett's fiction.

My favorite album by The Fall remains 1980's

Grotesque, the title of which neatly summarizes Mark E. Smith's approach to satire. The creation of grotesques depends upon exaggeration (i.e., pushing people, institutions, ideologies, arguments, and situations to their irrational extremes). This technique is of course at the heart of satire as an artistic tool. In a 2006 interview with Mo Ali, Aylett proffered the following definition: "Good satire uses people's own flawed or dishonest arguments against them by accelerating the argument into a sort of mind bomb." Satire aims to produce truth, to defend reason, but it cannot accomplish this without first deliberately distorting, deranging, and damaging our *ideological representations* of reality. The real world as such is, to quote the title of one of The Fall's finest albums, both "wonderful and frightening." This is why satire is also closely allied to surrealism and hyperrealism, both of which are central to Aylett's work.

The Fall originated in the bleak, post-industrial wasteland that was northern Britain in the late 1970s where drugs, violence, and environmental degradation were endemic. For MES, reality already *was* grotesque. In order to accurately express that truth in an artistic way, he had to parody and mock its ugliness, stupidity, and hypocrisy—to exaggerate ideological representations of reality into the realm of grotesquerie. His bitingly funny lyrics both condemned and reveled in his "northern gothic" cultural milieu. The Fall's artistic masterpiece is probably 1982's *Hex Enduction Hour*, a caustic send-up of British culture from top to bottom. MES and The Fall always positioned themselves as countercultural outsiders whose marginal identity and placement on the fringes of mainstream society allowed them to ironically observe and judge it in its totality—especially its class system.

Grotesquerie also entails a certain rejection of bourgeois realism and its codes of representation and narration. Satire understands that mimetic realism is not normative. Rather, it is an ideological category particular to capitalist society and to the bourgeois status or aspirations of its consumers. The "lowbrow" proletarian genres of speculative fiction are perfect vehicles for satirical writing.

To my knowledge, few rock critics have appreciated and discussed MES's brilliance as a narrative songwriter other than Taylor Parkes, whose excellent 2010 article in the online music magazine *The Quietus*, "The Fall and Mark E. Smith as a Narrative Lyric Writer," serves as a near-definitive survey of this subject. But MES's stories subvert the narrative codes of realism; they are highly fragmented and oblique, delirious mash-ups of existentialism, absurdism, and proletarian social realism with science fiction, fantasy, horror, and noir crime fiction. MES had a gift for bizarre imagery (perhaps related to his genuine belief in the supernatural), and many of The Fall's classic songs fall squarely into the genre of visionary weird fiction.

Steve Aylett's entire career has been a forceful rejection of bourgeois realism, which he derides not only for being useless and boring, but also for its reactionary nature. He uses grotesquerie to comment on the structural violence and human cruelty inherent in our surrounding world. Moreover, he demonstrates how that violence and cruelty crush honest and independent thought. On a formal level, Aylett is a remarkable and fractal-dense prose stylist; his sentences continually shatter and reconstruct the English language into new, kaleidoscopically colorful configurations.

In the narrative content of his books, Aylett goes

even further and eschews conventional, commercial genre fiction as well as bourgeois realism. His Beerlight series and the Accomplice quartet—and perhaps also *Shamanspace* (2001) and *Fain the Sorcerer* (2006)—could be read as burlesques or détournements of science fiction and fantasy, respectively, demonstrating how unoriginal and unimaginative those genres really are in practice. Aylett's books, by contrast, do not restrain their excess of weirdness and grotesquerie, much like the music of The Fall. The cognitive maps of contemporary (bourgeois) literary criticism cannot yet incorporate or even comprehend fiction as strange and original as Aylett's despite his work being classic satire at its core.

I consider Aylett's masterpieces to be his metafictional novel *Lint* and its companion piece, the faux-anthology *And Your Point Is?* (2006). *Lint* purports to be the biography of the obscure cult writer Jeff Lint, whose life amounts to a secret history of the twentieth century. The novel is as densely imbricated with jokes, weirdness, scorn and blame as Aylett's earlier work, and the prose remains wildly inventive, but these elements are better integrated into the story, better grounded in lived experience. *Lint* guides us along the title character's career (or lack thereof) as he draws his own unique lines of flight from pulp science fiction, beat poetry, performance art, the film and television industry, political conspiracy theories, underground comics, experimental theater, spiritual experiences, and psychedelic rock music. Each chapter provides countless opportunities for Aylett to describe (in miniature) selected works from Lint's fictional oeuvre, which is so fascinating, innovative, and funny that most readers fervently wish that Lint was not imaginary but *real*. The book is a comic inferno that subjects the culture industry to merciless and thoroughly deserved ridicule while critiquing political economy and uncovering buried and forgotten historical possibilities for the future of fantastic art. If one's aim is to suppress imagination and originality in every domain of existence, then the hegemony of the conventional—an aesthetic vacuum—is more effective than censorship.

Mark E. Smith's musical career has been, like Lint's fiction, a war against banality and conformity. Aylett depicts Jeff Lint's personality in a fashion strikingly similar to MES's artistic persona: MES, one might say, is the ur-Lint. Lint and MES have a perverse genius for effortlessly inciting other people to rage and resentment, whether through their satire—as Aylett says, "accelerating [flawed or dishonest arguments] into a sort of mind bomb"—or with their surreal, anarchic rebellions against conventional modes of thought, behavior, work, and speech. Both men are mercurial trickster archetypes, incapable of following authority or conforming to the received opinions of the masses. They succeed with regard to the only artistic criterion that matters: *a fidelity to aesthetic and political truth.*

Works Cited

Aylett, Steve. Interview by Mo Ali. *MoKnowChrome: Mo Ali-Words + Pictures.* 2006. Web. 17 Feb 2014.

Smith, Mark E. Interview by Taylor Parkes. *The Quietus.* "The Fall and Mark E. Smith as a Narrative Lyric Writer." 2010. Web. 17 Feb 2014.

The Fall. "Just Step Sideways." *High Priest and*

Kamerads. Beggars Banquet, 1982. MP3.

———. "Intro." *Totale's Turns.* Dojo Limited, 2013. CD

Jeff Lint, Rock Auteur

Michael Norris

On reading the first chapters of Steve Aylett's fictional biography, *Lint* (2005), I was struck by the word pairings that Aylett used for Jeff Lint's book titles (e.g., "*Nose Furnace*," "*Jelly Result*," "*The Phosphorus Tarot of Matchbooks*"). They reminded me of the names of songs and albums by Captain Beefheart and his Magic Band. Captain Beefheart (Don Van Vliet) was also fond of absurdist and surrealist titles (e.g., "Trout Mask Replica," "Bat Chain Puller," "Ice Cream for Crow").

Van Vliet's reputation as a harsh taskmaster is a 1960s legend. He and his band lived in a communal house in the Woodland Hills section of Los Angeles, and rehearsed *Trout Mask Replica* for eight months of 14-hour-a-day sessions. There were stories of verbal abuse and physical violence by Beefheart. In Chapter 20 of *Lint*, "Swaying Fast is Rocking," we discover that Lint took control of a band called the Unofficial Smile Group, and in between episodes of bizarre hazing, wrote "an album full of songs" that the band recorded and released as *The Energy Draining Church Bazaar* (149). Among other things, Lint established "Damage Night," bursting in on the sleeping band at four a.m. "dressed as the devil" and screaming (151).

In an April 2006 interview, Aylett confirmed that "*The Energy Draining Church Bazaar* sessions were inspired by the rehearsals for Beefheart's *Trout Mask Replica* . . . plus some 13th Floor Elevators" (Taylor).

One can see the similarity between the 13th Floor Elevators' psychedelic album covers and the cover of Aylett's fictional album. Keep in mind, these are long-play vinyl records, with covers large enough to display vibrant kaleidoscopic artwork, liner notes, and lyrics, especially on gatefold albums that opened up to twice the size of a regular album.

Aylett then captures another penchant of the age—the attempt by listeners to decipher the strange lyrics on albums and find messages in the liner notes. And, in some cases, interpret them in very dark ways. In a send-up of Charles Manson-like song interpretation leading to violence, Aylett writes: "Charismatic psychopath John Dyche claimed to have heard voices in 'Would You Mind Not Doing That' ordering him to carve a totem pole out of Peter Fonda, a task it is uncertain he achieved" (*Lint* 155).

The fact that the Unofficial Smile Group lived communally reminded me not only of Beefheart's band, but also of the band Love, who lived together in a house in Los Angeles that they called the Castle, and recorded their masterpiece *Forever Changes* amidst heavy drug use and the disintegration of the band. In Aylett's book, life at the Unofficial Smiles Group's house takes on cult-like properties. The band adopts the use of Lint neologisms like "spile" and "trun." The drummer, David Owen describes "a groupie injecting 'brimstone endorphin' directly into her forehead and saying . . . 'Spiders manage without us and wires don't care. An argument against'" (150).

Besides writing the lyrics for *The Energy Draining Church Bazaar*, Lint also shaped the band's sound. In a send-up of Beefheart-style musical direction, Lint says "I want a sound like a hot moon bursting like a bubble and dropping atom-size hens in the sea" (149), a sound which band member "Judge" Pete Fox creates by "hitting a melon with a frypan while letting out a sort of keening wail" (150).

The name Unofficial Smile Group (as well as a later chapter on Lint's theater work) brought to mind another 60's act called "The Hello People," a group from New York that performed in mime makeup and sang politically charged songs. "Hello" and "smile"— these upbeat words triggered the association. Even more than The Hello People, the name reminded me of the Beach Boys' concept album *Smile* and its tangled history.

Recording sessions for *Smile* began after the release of The Beach Boys' 1966 album *Pet Sounds*, a tour de force of Brian Wilson's genius in arranging and studio engineering. After hiring Van Dyke Parks to write lyrics, Wilson placed a grand piano in a sandbox in his living room, bought copious amounts of marijuana, hashish, and LSD, and went to work on what was intended to be a collection of songs that were thematically linked to the concept of Americana (thus the term "concept album"). The stress of following *Pet Sounds* may have taken its toll on the reportedly unstable Wilson, who eventually abandoned the project. Subsequent plans to release the album in 1972 and again in 1989 were never realized. In 2004, Wilson arranged a version of *Smile* that he performed solo on stage. He released a record album of the live performance. From time to time, bootleg versions of various *Smile* tracks from the original sessions appeared. Then, in 2011, Wilson released *The Smile Sessions*, a disc set of what the original *Smile* might have sounded like.

This brings us to the term "concept album" on which every song contributes to an overall theme or unified story. There is no clear marker for the appearance of the first concept album, and not everyone agrees on what constitutes one. Woody Guthrie's *Dust Bowl Ballads* (1940) consists of songs about the hardships of American migrant workers. Frank Sinatra's *Come Fly With Me* (1958) is a collection of songs about travel. But it was 1960s progressive rock bands seeking mind expansion, experimental art, and "happenings"—paired with 1960s pop bands in their quest for the next big thing—that produced an explosion of concept albums. These include The Moody Blues' *Days of Future Past* (1967), The Who's rock opera *Tommy* (1969), The Bee Gees' *Odessa* (1969), and several entries by The Alan Parsons Project, including the Poe-inspired *Tales of Mystery and Imagination* (1976) and the Asimov-inspired *I Robot* (1977).

Pink Floyd's chart-topping concept album *Dark Side of the Moon* (1973) explores the conflicts that tend to derail humanity (e.g., greed, war, the prospect of running out of time, mental illness). The subject of mental illness was related to the plight of founding Pink Floyd member Syd Barrett, who left the band in 1968 due to a nervous breakdown. Barrett's drug-fueled misadventures have taken on the same mythic quality of Philip K. Dick's so-called "religious experience" upon which Aylett based Lint's "fantastic lemon experience." In fact, the drug scandals and meltdowns of rock stars has become a cliché—and, for Aylett, a vehicle for satirizing this late sixties zeitgeist.

Works Cited

Aylett, Steve. *Lint*. New York: Thunder's Mouth Press, 2005.

Taylor, Justin. "An Interview with Steve Aylett." *Bookslut*. July 2006. Web. 17 May 2013.

Aylett at the End of Time

Bill Ectric

There is a Silver Age comic book panel showing
Wonder Woman flying her invisible jet plane over the
Ionic temples of her island homeland. It is a sleek line
drawing by Ross Andru. The sand, sea, and sky are
inked in soft blues and browns by Mike Esposito. In
my mind's eye, I saw that illustration when I read the
first sentence in Steve Aylett's book, *Rebel at the End of
Time*, "Regina Sparks flew over a lion-coloured desert
in a monoplane of clear glass" (Rebel 7). Maybe my
mind's eye drew upon an awareness of Aylett's frequent
forays into the comic book world. I was surprised to
learn that "lion" is actually an official color designated
as #C19A6B by the ISCC-NBS System of Color
Description.

    Rebel at the End of Time takes place in a universe
created by groundbreaking science fiction writer
Michael Moorcock, who wrote a series of novels and
short stories known collectively as the Dancers at the
End of Time series. The people who inhabit this series
are simply whiling away the time before the universe
collapses upon itself. They entertain themselves by
throwing parties and playing games in which they
constantly change themselves and their environment by
the use of power rings (another comic book reference:
Green Lantern). Fads come and go faster than ever.
Romance is almost extinct, but not quite.

Aylett's *Rebel* is a reversal of the romantic relationship dynamic that ran through all three novels in Michael Moorcock's trilogy *Dancers at the End of Time* (1993, Orion/Gollancz). In *Dancers*, a young lady from Victorian England, Amelia Underwood, travels to the future and is appalled by a world where actions have no consequences, work is unnecessary, and people engage in free sex without shame or self-consciousness. Much of the plot revolves around her relationship with a young man she meets in the future named Jherek Carnelian, who is good-natured but does not understand concepts like virtue and restraint.

In Rebel, a young 21st man named Leo del Toro roars into the end-of-time future on a motorcycle. He arrives in the midst of an elaborate festival. The Duke of Queens, a character borrowed from the Moorcock books, has created a full-size Egyptian pyramid as the centerpiece of his latest public amusement. The Duke's protégé is the aforementioned girl in the invisible airplane, Regina Sparks, who develops a relationship with Leo, the rebel motorcyclist. Leo cannot help but notice Regina. Among the flamboyantly attired revelers, including some who have shape-shifted beyond human form, Regina's costume of choice is no costume at all. She prefers to be naked, her snow-white skin "patterned black tattoos of twisted vines" (*Rebel* 7).

The attraction between Regina and Leo stands out as the most fully realized romance in any of Aylett's books, and he writes it brilliantly. Chapter 10 finds Regina asleep in "a bedroom of domino patterning and Russian lacquer furniture, under a dreamcatcher like a cartoon spider web" (96). The dreamcatcher is a perfect touch. One part organic handcrafted art and one part satellite dish. Originated by the Ojibwe tribe of Native Americans (also known as Chippewa) and later

70

commercialized by the arts & crafts industry, dreamcatchers were said to filter out bad dreams and allow good ones to into our sleeping psyche. With that in mind, Regina's dreamcatcher can be just another fad, like the Duke of Queen's pyramid, or a glimpse into her humanity and femininity. Even at the end of time, with its overall lack of sentiment, a girl still adorns her room with whimsical accessories. Not a stuffed animal, jewelry tree, or unicorn poster – she has a dreamcatcher, sieving ancient dreams as they gust across the expanse of space and time.

Regina is dreaming of a conversation with Leo. The dream is filled with black and white imagery: off-white statues, a charcoal landscape, and black tears. At first, Leo aroused her curiosity because he is an anomaly, but as the conversation progresses, she finds herself attracted to him, not really understanding the emotion except in her subconscious, which is the dream. His pessimism is strange to her, but it registers at some level, as a sign of life.

Meanwhile, in the real world, while Regina sleeps, the dreamcatcher above her bursts into flames, which is simultaneously the spark of love, the eternal flame, and the heartbreak of it; because to fully accept Leo, she must acknowledge his world view, which is basically that "somewhere in time... suffering still exists – perhaps all the more if it was never recognized or remedied" (97). Conversely, Regina seems to have done what the rebel Leo strives for, to throw off the shackles of oppression and be free. But to Leo, the freedom achieved by Regina and her friends at the end of time is shallow and sad, because it's meaningless and without consequence. Anything they do can be redone if the outcome isn't satisfactory.

After the dream, the next time Leo del Toro and Regina Sparks see one another, her black vine tattoos on snow white skin have been replaced by a riot of colors. She explains, "You... made me blush," (139). The budding connection between Leo and Regina presents a striking contrast to pyrotechnic liaison between Rosa and Dante 2 in Aylett's much earlier book, *Slaughtermatic*, which includes the passage, "Rosa raked her steel-plated nails into his chest and he ripped between agony and glory like a flashbulb...the walls were peeling like a pearl, strobing behind Rosa's tossing head. Rosa was yelling ballistic technicalities each time she sank onto him, her face gnashy and flushed" (Aylett, *Slaughtermatic*).

In Voltaire's masterpiece, *Candide* (1759), the protagonist meets and converses with a variety of characters along the path of his journey. Voltaire uses these encounters to introduce and satirize diverse belief systems, both secular and religious. In much the same way, Aylett devotes certain chapters of *Rebel* to discussions between Leo and characters created by Michael Moorcock. Leo discusses revolution with Li Pao, religion with Doctor Volospion, and sorrow with Werther de Goethe.

In Aylett's book, Li Pao introduces himself as an "officer of the 27th century's People's Republic" (Rebel 101). Moorcock apparently styled Li Pao as a Chairman Mao type of revolutionary and "added some trade union rhetoric that was widespread in the United Kingdom during the 1970s, when Moorcock wrote most of the *End of Time* stories and novels" (Aylett. "RE: *Rebel.*"). In contrast, Leo del Toro is more like the popular *Motorcycle Diary* version of Che Guevara, with more than a passing nod to James Dean (Aylett. "RE: *Rebel.*"). They are both in danger of becoming rebels without a cause. Aylett's version of Li Pao is more cynical than Moorcock's version. Pao tells Leo that, at most, revolutions may improve conditions temporarily, but progress has and always will be "halted by lack and emergency" (Rebel, 108). In other words, expected changes for the better are constantly interrupted when the peoples' energies are consumed with survival and sustenance (lack), or when they become frightened by real or imagined attacks from outside their country, allowing the powers-that-be to put all progressive change on hold to "protect" the populace militarily (emergency). Leo realizes that Li Pao's beliefs were "mental decoration, not meant to be applied" (109).

Doctor Volospion, another Moorcock character, guides Leo on a tour through his museum of religious artifacts, even though, writes Aylett, "to Volospion's mind the notion that faith should require paraphernalia seemed a contradiction" (113). Some of the references are obvious; others are abstract and impressionistic. The "hinged wooden stack which unfolded to show three faded pictures" (113-114) is obviously a triptych, and the people in each picture with "melons balanced on their heads" (114) are most likely depictions of saints with halos. The "round Calamity Bible" (114) is a more general image. Perhaps all the calamities are printed in red. That would make for a bloody text.

Moorcock's melancholy creation, Werther de Goethe, has named himself after the protagonist from Johann Wolfgang von Goethe's novel, *The Sorrows of Young Werther* (1774). Johann Goethe was part of the German Sturm und Drang literary movement, which emphasized turbulent emotions. One might compare it to the 20th Century music genre called Emo. Sensing Leo's trepidation at the prospect of living in a world without goals or meaning, Werther invites the Rebel to join him "in the heady glare of the constant end" (Rebel, 92) and, "Leave your hopes behind" (92). Leo's encounter with Werther contains some of Aylett's most poetic, exhilarating, and dichotomous observations.

"I was born into this hearse of ribs," says Werther, "surrounded already with these worn curses: the incomprehensible skeleton of history, tribal authority bound by a thin bit of cosmic fortune…this world is a doorknob that spins without engaging…the smallest conceivable portion of time supplies us with ample tragedy for a lifetime… each tear contains a hologram of its cause" (92-93)

Werther seems almost gleeful in his pursuit of misery. Like the 18th Century Sturm und Drang devotees, he embraces angst as fashion. But what state of mind drew him to such morbidity in the first place? Game or not, dwelling on doom and despair is bound to affect his outlook. He and Leo are among the few people at the end of time that were born naturally rather than created artificially, and perhaps this helps them understand one another. Werther says, "Despair is honest," (92) and while Leo does not especially like Werther's misery, at least he can relate to it. After all, a person becomes a rebel when they are unhappy with the way things are. Leo is moved to participate in the conversation, as best he can, by quoting an old adage from his past, "The winners write the histories," and adds "but only if they can be bothered," (93-94) referring to the cavalier attitude he has encountered at the end of time. Leo's brief but honest effort to engage in conversation is enough to prompt Werther to proffer a hope of sorts, even if couched in melancholia. "Over time," he tells Leo, "failure makes a structure. Any structure can be used to climb" (96).

Misery and humor shape Aylett's books like two sides of a planet. Like Voltaire, Aylett sees problems and contradictions that, to him, are obvious, and he is baffled when everyone acts as though nothing were wrong.

Discussing his childhood, Aylett once told me in an email:

> **If I could see that someone had just contradicted them self, I would stare at them with what I thought was pointed and arch expectation, because I was sure they'd realize their error immediately. To me it would be visual, like a huge bit of modern sculpture in the room with us, impossible to miss. But they wouldn't notice their mistake, and as far as they were concerned they'd said something reasonable and this five-year-old was just staring gormlessly at them. This got me a reputation as a moron, or as 'vague' (Aylett. "RE: Beginnings").**

Voltaire must have felt the same way when he spoke his mind to Chevalier de Rohan at a dinner party, only to be beaten up by Rohan's servants (Shelley, 40-41), and then to be laughed at for getting beat up (Aldridge). Of course, some seventy years later, the misuses of power by the French aristocracy culminated in the Reign of Terror. Things simmer for a long time before they erupt. This goes back to Aylett's concept of the creepchannel.

Featured in the four books of his Accomplice series, the creepchannel is a system of ethereal tunnels used by demons for transportation. Aylett says the creepchannel consists of compressed energy from "all the agony that is denied, evaded, or ignored in society, or for that matter, in life. All that negativity has to go somewhere, just as it has to come out somewhere. You'll notice it has the same feel as Doctor Skychum's vision in my short story 'Gigantic'." (Aylett, "RE: Beginnings"). He further describes the creepchannel as having a "layout roughly based on a migraine pattern… like the sick nerve pattern that visually can sometimes appear, also the blind spots that can happen sometimes (as with the way the creepchannel entrance or exit is sometimes remembered and sometimes not) and the general sick feeling of the creepchannel" (Aylett, RE: Beginnings). This brings to mind Jean-Paul Sartre's *Nausea*, that lost and disorientated feeling in the face of a seemingly meaningless and absurd world.

In an interview for "Fiend Magazine" Martyn Pedler quotes Aylett as saying that "satire never really changes anything" (Pedler). Aylett elaborates with "I've said somewhere before that everyone knows what's a real crime, everyone understands what is unjust, irrespective of legislation. But few people have the courage or energy to do anything about it, because the worst criminals have such massive power. They have armies, and they have the law" (Pedler).

Jeff Lint, the title character of Aylett's mockumentary, Lint is an entertaining amalgamation of celebrity writers and artists including Philip K. Dick, Kurt Vonnegut, Hunter S. Thompson, Captain Beefheart, the Beat writers, and others, but Aylett has also said that "There's a fair bit of me in Lint obviously" (Taylor).

Summing up the fictional Jeff Lint's philosophy, in the last chapter of *Lint,* Aylett writes, "Satire was like scrubbing tombstones with a toothbrush, but honorable none-the-less," (Lint 196) and that "the inhabitants of this world complain in vain, but this is no reason to cease stating the truth" (196). Aylett told Richard Marshall that satire "has no real effect on anything structurally in actual life …I really think you change the outside world more by painting a fence than by writing satire, but I still think the truth has inherent value, even if nobody hears it" (Marshall). This explains why Aylett's book, Lint, while predominately a work of humor, ends with the cryptic assertion that Jeff Lint sought to "unearth the bruises underground" (Lint 198). These "bruises," like the accumulated negative energy of the creepchannel, must ultimately come to light.

Richard Holmes, in his book *Sidetracks: Explorations of a Romantic Biographer*, writes:

> **For Voltaire, the essence of intellectual freedom was wit...enlightenment and also a certain kind of laughter: The laughter that distinguishes man from the beasts. But it is not a simple kind of laughter: It is also close to tears. Voltaire's symbolic grin (as we begin to examine it) contains both these elements when he surveys the human condition. Life amuses and delights him; but it also causes him pain and grief. (Holmes 346)**

In light of the above quote, we might say that "Voltaire's symbolic grin" represents both a mirthful smile and a grimace of pain. The tragedy/comedy masks.

So, does Aylett offer any hope amidst the dystopian violence of Beerlight, the Kafkaesque lunacy of Accomplice, or the meaningless flippancy of his and

Moorcock's End of Time scenario? Let us examine that question.

The dancers at the end of time often misconstrue events and customs from their distant past. The eons have dimmed their understanding and garbled the words of their ancestors. The ancient Roman phrase, "Remember you are but a man" becomes "Remember you are butter, man" (Aylett, "RE: Rebel"). The Egyptian "coffin chamber" becomes "coughing chamber" (Rebel 15). Sometimes they get it partly correct. For example, Regina describes an Egyptian pyramid as machine for processing the death of kings. The Duke of Queens, explaining the extravaganza he has planned, says that he will be:

> **ritually killed upon the summit of this pyramid of mine, then conveyed downward into a coughing chamber within, and a gigantic golden replica of my face emerges from the front of the building. This sacred face makes the surrounding land fertile, a jungle grows up around the edifice, and the entire scene becomes the stuff of legend" (15).**

Only Lord Jagged seems to have a sense of continuity. This is because he is a time traveler. He has "been around" as the saying goes. Living in different times has given him wisdom that is lacking in most of his associates. Aylett said in an email:

> **I think Lord Jagged is the wisest of the Dancers - not always right about things, but more aware of the fact that there is something else other than the Dancers'**

**facades and fancies. This is enhanced by
the fact that he has access to (and later
travels to) other times. You can see with
Jagged that he changes 'modes' - he drops
the florid Dancers act and becomes a more
sober person when alone or when speaking
to someone who understands (Aylett. "RE:
Rebel").**

In Rebel, Lord Jagged has an inscription over the
door to his castle that says, "Save the heart" (173). I
find a double meaning in this phrase. Beginning with
the pyramid created by the Duke of Queens, the book
contains numerous references to ancient Egyptian
customs. Historians tell us that during the course of
mummification, all internal organs were removed and
treated by a process intended to preserve them. The
organs were placed in separate containers, all except for
the heart. Before wrapping the body in linen, they
placed the heart back into the chest. As in many
cultures, the ancient Egyptians believe that the heart
contained one's intelligence, emotion, and soul.

I asked Aylett in an email to elaborate on his
phrase, "save the heart." He replied:

**It's really about preserving & reminding
oneself of what one loves and believes, &
thereby maintaining a center. You could
see it like Gurdjieff's belief that people are
not born with a soul but that through
great effort one can be created, or see it
like the useful awareness of what you
actually like, love and believe, and what is
merely inherited, assumes or decreed
from elsewhere - this can be viewed**

> visually like a landscape. All these meanings overlap. I didn't consciously have mummification in mind, even though I did later mention that in my book *Heart of the Original*. I'm talking about the living heart and its authenticity (Aylett. "RE: *Rebel*").

Voltaire said, "I get what I get from my brain, but one's brain is soon dried up. It is only the heart that is inexhaustible" (Nemeth).

Rebel at the End of Time is populated by a combination of characters created by Michael Moorcock for his *End of Time* series and additional characters created by Steve Aylett. Aylett also added some locations that were not in the Moorcock stories, such as Hapexian Wasteland, Volospion's Museum, and Conception Junction. The people who inhabit Michael Moorcock's *Dancers-at-the-End-of-Time* Universe use advanced technology (housed in power rings) to alter their appearance and create amazing life forms; therefore, it is a perfect canvas for Aylett to paint his broad, exaggerated, and visually oriented descriptions. In Aylett's world, an end-of-time soiree is "a throng of snouts, wings and tails" (Rebel 7). A city "creaks with corners, clotted in darkness" (140). A red velveteen panther named Masha la Mash is accompanied by a sentient, nine-foot tall coat-of-arms, "its openwork biology evidencing a quickened heart rate and firing cynapses" (151). Orpington hens learn "to fly underwater like sunfish" (142).

To conclude this essay, here is a guide listing which "end-of-time" characters were created by Aylett and which were created by Moorcock.

AYLETT'S CHARACTERS

Regina Sparks
Leo del Toro
Whisper Terrible
Principal Krill
Fox Grave
Baron Coma
Again the Shuttle Clue
Jack-in-the-Green
Quoi Vico
Profumo the Monkey
Falcomatis of the Jet Black Trauma Feathers
Bone Quixote
Roxanne Ansari
Ulysses the Overwhale
The Luton Clown
Pastor Bulbous
Masha la Mash
Zinn

MOORCOCK'S CHARACTERS

Duke of Queens
Bishop Castle
Iron Orchid
Doctor Volospion
Jherek Carnelian
Lord Jagged
Argonheart Po
Brannart Morphail
Li Pao
Corporal Pork
My Lady Charlotina
Mistress Christia

> Werther de Goethe
> Lord Shark
> O'Kala Incarnadine
> Sweet Orb Mace
> The Earl of Carbolic
> Gaf the Horse in Tears

Works Cited

Aldridge, Alfred Owen. Voltaire and the Century of Light. New Jersey: Princeton University Press, 1975. Princeton Legacy Library. Ebook.

--- *Lint*. New York: Thunder's Mouth Press, 2005. Print.

--- *Rebel at the End of Time*. UK: Scar Garden Press, 2012. Print.

--- *Slaughtermatic*. UK: Scar Garden Press, 2011. Kindle Ebook.

Aylett, Steve. "Re: Beginnings." Message to Bill Ectric. 14 July 2013. E-mail.

Aylett, Steve. "Re: *Rebel*." Message to Bill Ectric. 18 December 2014. Email.

Elliott, Luke. "Goaste," interview by Luke Elliott. Web http://razstar.brinkster.net/goaste/wordsinterviews.html

Holmes, Richard. *Sidetracks: Explorations of a Romantic Biographer*. New York: Vintage, 2001.

Marshall, Richard. "An Interview with Steve Aylett."
    3:AM Magazine. 2002. Web. 12 Dec. 2013

Nemeth, Alexander J. *Voltaire's Tormented Soul: A
    Psychobiological Inquiry.* Bethlehem, PA: Lehigh
    University Press. 1 Feb. 2008.

Pedler, Martyn. "Steve Aylett Interviewed." Fiend
    Magazine. 2005. Wed. 2 Feb. 2013.

Shelley, Mary Wollstonecraft. *Lives of the Most Eminent
    French Writers.* Philadelphia: Lea and Blanchard,
    1840. Harvard College Library.

Taylor, Justin. "An Interview with Steve Aylett."
    Bookslut. July 2006. Web. 11 Jan. 2015

Satire, Anxiety, and Prospect in *The Caterer*

Andrew Wenaus

"When the issue is to put into language something which has never yet been spoken, then everything depends on whether language gives or withholds the appropriate word."
—Martin Heidegger

"Certainly the Caterer's friends are bewildered (or understanding) enough to stand listening to this drivel."
—Steve Aylett

In *Karloff's Circus* (2004), Aylett writes that "the only puzzle worth doing is one which notices when it's solved—something is activated" (*The Complete Accomplice* 316). Aylett's satire is explicitly purposeful, even classical. Yet his work is puzzling. It reveals itself as that which, if solved, will activate a kind of intense scrutiny: after reading Aylett, our own assumptions and biases undergo revision. A satirist and trickster, Aylett assumes the role of a contemporary social critic, a provocateur, and a defender of the honesty and ethics in aesthetic enterprise. Provocation in Aylett's writing, however, achieves an affect so unworldly that its significance may blind readers by its own sheer radiance.

While the content of much of Aylett's work is preoccupied with the abuses and arbitrariness of authority that has "no moral weight that stands up to a moment's scrutiny, and [that] is enforced by the threat of violence" (Ectric, "Interview"), it is the manner through which he accuses and disapproves (of) the contemporary state of the arts that makes him remarkable. In this sense, Aylett's satire is like the "effortless incitement," he attributes to Jeff Lint in *Lint,* "so startling that people . . . flinch and forget what they [are] saying" (*Lint* 10). His pessimism is oddly constructive in its impulse. Such dissension ultimately results in something strikingly similar to what Martin Heidegger calls *angst* or anxiety: that which tears one from common experience and lays bare one's concerns and prejudices. This experience unveils a new context-specific space of discussion characterized by an unusual disclosure through dissent. Amidst the dim aureole of recent literary achievement is Aylett's work shimmering at the fringes of contemporary fiction. In the end, this radiant space is where honesty and authenticity in both discussion and art are made possible.

Aylett entered the literary scene in 1994. He has since published thirteen novellas, two collections of short stories, a mock biography, a book of mock literary essays, and numerous comic strips. The vast majority of Aylett's critical acclaim comes from the admiration of fellow literary figures rather than from literary critics. Michael Moorcock suggests that Aylett is currently "the most original voice on the literary scene" (Aylett *Lint*) and he is likely accurate in his assessment. Grant Morrison also holds Aylett's work in high regard, "If you've been waiting for the first great neo-modernist novelist of the new century," Morrison writes, "your wait is now over" (Morrison). Alan Moore, in his introduction to Aylett's novella *Fain the Sorcerer* (2006), suggests that, not only is Aylett "very,

86

very funny," he is also "one of the most exciting and innovative creators to emerge in a long time" (Moore viii). So, Aylett is in good company and rightly so: he is a writer's writer, relentless, and an uncompromising master of style. A virtuoso of epigraph and aphorism, his prose is remarkably compressed. The *Complete Review* notes that:

> **Aylett's short little books are in a league of their own. Only Will Self displays a similar sharp humour coupled with such great attention to language and expression, but where Self burrows himself into his flights of fancy, Aylett is almost an epigrammatist. This is writing so lean that the sentences seem individually chiseled and then set, like bricks in a wall, next to each other. Not always ideal for structuring a narrative, but Aylett still manages to grab and hold the reader's attention. The sharp, dark wit, utter hopelessness (with little oppressive despair), and unlikely events Aylett presents make for unusual reads. Aylett builds (and collapses) worlds...with a few words, meticulously wrought rough sketches flung at the reader . . . [He] aims to entertain with his bizarre and decidedly surreal writing, and by and large he succeeds. ("Steve Aylett at the *Complete Review*")**

This aptitude, marked by his adherence to stylistic precision, intimates baroque ornamentation—Moore calls him, rather than a brick mason, "a jeweler" of the "most finely chiseled gems" (Moore, "Introduction" viii)—whereby a great deal of intricate and painstakingly crafted detail is condensed into very little narrative space. And such stylistic adornment lends itself to the intricate ways in which the patterning of Aylett's prose seems to operate almost independently from the plot itself, giving his work a multi-dimensional quality. "There are several threads of sense going through [the phrasing] at different depths," Aylett writes, "I think the mind picks up which bits link in to which other bits. Some's almost a subliminal sort of thing going on, and then at the simplest level there's the running gags or repetitions like the 'Snail, Sarge' conversation, which is just so stupid I really like it. And if you don't like all that there's always the story to fall back on" (Ectric, "Interview with Steve Aylett"). The plot content of Aylett's work is, much like his style, strange and, as Moore remarks, very, very funny. That is, a notable quality of Aylett's fiction is in the way the content and style are indelibly interdependent and, yet, the epigrammatic precision of his prose can operate in striking ways, leaping up from the diegesis of the plot towards another level of meaning altogether. This is epigram at its finest and yet at its most innovative. That is, his writing expresses witticism and truism with striking and amusing turns in its meaning at the level of epigram and, yet, this operative mode also works at the level of narrative: sentences, the epigram itself, takes a surprising turn away from, not the subject of the sentence, but the diegetic structure itself.

Resultantly, Aylett's prose can be remarkably abstract, resulting in rather opaque plots. However, funny as these plots are, they are certainly not to the author's detriment. Moorcock remarks:

Andrew Wenaus

> **You can't afford to skip through Aylett's idiosyncratic eloquence . . . Aylett's language is often the substance, the narrative. You are lost unless you accept the logic of his characters, the sardonic rhythms of his prose...By the end of the book it all seems perfectly logical, while the world around you is definitely askew. This is his genius. (Moorcock).**

Aylett's prose alternates between intensely compressed meaning and what might be considered mock epigrams and nonsense aphorisms. And it is with this point that we may qualify Moorcock's argument that the language in Aylett's work is the substance and the narrative rather than the plot. The unpredictable alternations in his prose between highly semantically packed epigrams and sentences that appear syntactically and phonologically to be profound but which are, in actuality, humorous nonsense, may indeed be Aylett's comment on the difficulty of the reader to distinguish stupidity from honesty, convention from innovation. Again, the procedure here is satirical: pushing convention to grotesque extremes, eschewing tradition and expectation altogether, utilizing science fiction and fantasy tropes mockingly in a parodic way, demonstrating the systematic absurdity of authoritative institution through slapstick routines—or what D. Harlan Wilson calls "splatterschtick" (Ectric "Inside the Head of D. Harlan Wilson") - Aylett's aims are the aims of classical satire: "Everything humanity does, its wishes, fear, anger, pleasures, joys, runnings to and fro, form the medley of my book" writes Juvenal (Juvenal *Satires* I). After reading Aylett, akin to reading classical satire, "the world around you is definitely askew" thus

89

prompting the reader to see, for the first time, everything humanity does in a new way.

Aylett is caustic and yet, along with this pessimism, he is calling for new and higher standards in both society and the arts. Moore, after all, remarks that "Aylett is in many ways a staunch traditionalist" (Moore, "Introduction" vii). "I enjoy parody and stupid stuff," Aylett notes, "but more often than not I'll use it as a housing for old-time satire, politics and bitter axe-grinding" (Ectric, "Interview with Steve Aylett"). What is so remarkable about Aylett's satire is the way it shocks a contemporary audience with its inexplicably odd and denaturalizing tendencies in similar ways that masterworks of satire achieved upon first publication. That is, Aylett does not seek to reproduce the conventions of content, style, and target of satire that are constituents of the literary cannon; instead, he aims to achieve the same effect that these works achieved upon publication. This explains why the modalities that propel Aylett's work must be unusual and strange. Wilson remarks that "Humor has less to do with the material than the author's personal taste and desires. Humor can be tricky, too, because it's so subjective, and there are so many different kinds, and it can be 'found' anywhere, even in the most dramatic contexts" (Ectric, "Inside"). Freud, in his *The Joke and Its Relation to the Unconscious* (1905) remarks that his own *Interpretation of Dreams* (1900), "may have produced more 'bafflement' than 'light dawning'" (Freud 154) among his colleagues suggesting that, even beyond the dramatic, mocking and ridicule are invited everywhere and that which may be taken as natural is, indeed, when considered from a novel point of view, hilarious despite its brilliance. Freud contends that jokes unveil our unconscious desire and he understands humor well enough to know that his own work is not immune from its own workings; here, we may accept this logic from both a satirical and phenomenological perspective in that humor reveals epistemological biases. Subjectivity of humor is certainly a point worthy of note: the bafflement and strangeness, the sometimes "stupid" or banal in Aylett's work serves to disclose the means in which no text or context is safe from ridicule. Aylett's humor and his satirical approach to fiction demands that the reader *see* the world and the arts as a kind of clearing that rests outside that which is sensible through convention and tradition. In an analogous way that Aylett uses the epigram at both a syntactic and narrative level, he employs the bafflement that accompanies authentic satirical writing by, not turning to his own work, but by creating the infuriatingly strange and funny Jeff Lint, a satirical depiction of an author whose work poses the reader with the contentions of authentic innovation: unintelligibility, banality, and the terrific significance of aesthetic possibility.

Aylett published *Lint* (2005), a humorous mock-biography of the imaginary author, Jeff Lint, a writer who authored inventive, eccentric, brilliant, and deranged works across an array of media from short stories, novels, film scripts, children's cartoons, to comics. Bill Ectric writes that "*Lint* is to literature what *Spinal Tap* is to heavy metal music: a brilliant send-up of anecdotal, cult-of-personality biographies." He continues "the parody swings freely between the sci-fi genre, the Beats, and classic pulp magazines. We follow a legendary author named Jeff Lint, who lived in the age when "dozens of new magazines appeared, with titles like *Astounding, Bewildering, Confusing, Baffling . . . Useless . . . Appalling, Made-Up . . . Thrilling Wonder Stories,* and *Swell Punch-Ups"* and editors would order up "an octopus, a spaceman, and a screaming woman" for the cover of a typical issue" (Ectric, "Interview"). The short lived comic book, *The Caterer*, marks Lint's catastrophic foray into the publishing scene of 1970s comics. The nine-issue run of *The Caterer* features the inexplicable adventures of Jack Marsden. The fictional illustrator of *The Caterer*, Brandon Sienkel, describes Marsden: "The Caterer was a strange one—he didn't have any special powers, he was this blond grinning college kid as far as I could make out. He sometimes pulled a gun. There just didn't seem to be [any rhyme or reason]…the character would fly into a rage about things. But it was strangely hypnotic, I must say. We had fan mail" (Aylett, *Lint* 111-12). The comic book is essentially plotless and is marked by surreal humor, non-sequiturs, and an overwhelming sense of confusion. In December 2008, Steve Aylett and Floating World Comics published a "reprint" of the third issue of *The Caterer* as a kind of companion piece to *Lint* and the book of mock criticism on Lint's fiction, *And Your Point Is?: Scorn & Meaning in Jeff Lint's Fiction* (2006). In a sense, the "reprint" is an extended metaphor that seizes, juxtaposes, and manipulates the comic book as a literary medium and by analogy invites critics to usurp, manipulate, and mediate upon the act of comic book criticism.

But *The Caterer #3* is more than simply a companion piece. It is, in its medium as a visual work, a kind of puzzle that, when considered in the proper configuration, discloses what the reader of Aylett's satirical project, even his complete oeuvre, should *see*. Indeed, as Aylett suggests in *Lint*, "tracing the Caterer's motives is a parlour game for Lint fans" (112) - which may be Aylett self-reflexively pestering the critic to examine the motivation behind examining experimental or avant-garde works of art that rest outside popular and academic affirmation. "Fans debate its motifs and catchphrases, and the Caterer's fogbound motivations," writes Aylett, "'I Believe Marsden represents Lint's own creative urge, bursting out at odd moments and killing everybody'" (Aylett, *Lint* 112). By juxtaposing finely crafted ridicule and censure with banality and illogicality readers may more readily recognize artificial parameters and biases in contemporary art and thought. Jonathan Swift famously identifies satire as:

a sort of glass wherein beholders do generally discover everybody's face but their own, which is the chief reason for that kind of reception it meets in the world, and that so very few are offended with it. But, if it should happen otherwise, the danger is not great; and I have learned, from long experience, never to apprehend mischief from those understandings I have been able to provoke: for anger and fury, though they add strength to the sinews of the body, yet are found to relax those of the mind, and to render all its efforts feeble and impotent. (Swift)

Aylett would likely agree with Swift. In his 2008 preface to *The Complete Accomplice*, Aylett articulates what might be considered his own definition of satire: "There persists a notion that humanity will learn lessons as a result of the upcoming collapses and that human denial has a limit (a notion mentally sustainable only because it doesn't)," writes Aylett. "In fact the best we find at land's end is a society where the considered life plan is still a choice of which exalted con-game to fall for" (Aylett, *The Complete Accomplice* 7). Yet, both assume the pose of the satirist; and, in the very act of writing within the genre in question, both wish to, rather than relax the mind, open the mind to the potentiality of making manifest alternatives. However, Aylett is not nearly as Cartesian as Swift: the anger and fury of the sinews are inevitably embedded in the discontent of the mind. Indeed, Aylett, like any satirist, wants the reader to discover his or her reflection in the glass; he would wish that the reader *see* how they are an accomplice to the folly of their time. And the print publication of *The Caterer #3*—a graphic medium—forces us into just that activity: we must *look* and *see* how Aylett's satire operates.

The cover of the third issue of *The Caterer* is typical for an action strip. There are missiles, explosions, a speeding car, a mountain ledge, some tombstones or ancient monoliths, and the overconfidently smirking (actually, psychotic) face of Jack Marsden.

Textually, the cover page is rather brilliant. There is the date and price of the issue in the top left corner, the stamp of (unlikely) approval by the Comics Code Authority in the top right corner. Aylett explains the means of producing the artwork and layout for the comic:

It all started out as samples from a lot of 1970s comics—that blonde grinning jock appears throughout those comics. Then I flipped them, changed colors, changed expressions and body positions, etc. and blended them into different backgrounds and with different characters, muted the colors down again, then added dialogue. Often I was doing so much re-drawing I

was virtually drawing the character from scratch, by the end. (Ectric, "Interview")

Aylett's sampling is not only reminiscent of the modernists and dada artists—Max Ernst's collage graphic narrative *Une semaine de bonté (1934)* comes to mind—but also cut-up experiments of William S. Burroughs and Brion Gysin. However, what Aylett is doing is part of a more recent movement in the literary arts: borrowing not only from the avant-garde traditions of modernist experimentation and the later cut-ups but also from music, literature, and remix. The techniques of sampling, manipulating, looping, and reconfiguring is what Paul D. Miller aka DJ Spooky calls rhythm science[1] and are notably practiced by Kathy Acker, Stewart Home, Graham Rawle, and Jeff Noon.[2] Miller describes rhythm science as "a mirror held up to a culture . . . that has released itself from the constraints of the ground to drift through dataspace, continuously morphing its form in response to diverse streams of information" (Miller 5). What Aylett is doing differently from the other authors practicing literary remix is using the mode as a strictly satirical enterprise. The mirror thus reflects culture just as satire reflects the follies of an age. Again, when we look at *The Caterer* we are gazing at a satirical representation of the cultural scene in which we inhabit. As a result, the pretext to the comic's title—"Try and try to justify"—gestures towards the satirical nature and tricksterism of Aylett's comic. This act of justification is the challenge of Aylett's satire: try to justify, try to *see* and interpret what the project sets out to accomplish; the reader will be baffled and surprised by the honesty of, not strictly the content, but the gesture. The hilarious title of the issue, "Jack Marsden Dials I for Inconvenience," reemphasizes the difficult task upon which a reader is about to embark.

Describing the plot of *The Caterer* would be both difficult and possibly pointless. It opens with a more or less meaningless, though quite funny, phone conversation between a shadow-faced man and the secretary of a Faculty Office: "Faculty office, how may I help you," the secretary asks. She is answered by a baffling request from Jack Marsden: "I need a coffee pot in the shape of my own severed head. The coffee should come out the nose or out a gill-like frown on the forehead. Pick me up by my ears. Do it. Pick me up by my ears." The voice on the phone continues: "And all these glories must be delivered in five of your Earth minutes. Yeah." To which the secretary interrupts, "This is the school faculty office, Sir." The interrupted man continues, "for reasons I think you know." And then the man delivers what might be considered the punch line to the absurd gag, "Wait, this isn't passport control?" In the third panel, one may expect, after the one-liner, the dialogue to develop into something more salient. However, the man's voice over the phone offers another non-sequitur, "Now where will I find someone who'll talk me down after I've had a shave?" (1). The remaining four panels on the first page consist of more humorous nonsense from Marsden. Marsden, amidst obscure aphoristic outbursts, begins addressing the secretary - without explanation - as "Mister Skeleton" (1). Ultimately, this strange introduction functions as a frame tale for the issue. The following page has Marsden walking in a grave yard with the captions "Three days earlier Jack Marsden steps out" (3). This marks the beginning of the story.

Again, attempting to describe the plot would be an obscure task to say the least. The general structure of the piece, however, shifts between the Sheriff Leonard Bayard's constant search for Jack Marsden (presumably for the purpose of incarceration), the various unpredictable conversations and exploits of Marsden, and exceptionally bizarre passages of Marsden in comical delirious hallucinations. The strip ends by returning to the frame tale, though this time we see the conversation from Marsden's end of the phone conversation—the building in which he converses is on fire—the final panel includes the burning building with a silhouette figure of Marsden.

Visually, to flip through the pages of *The Caterer* one gets the impression of an intriguingly bizarre action strip characterized by periodic scene changes, flashbacks, fight sequences, etc. There is one particularly strange sequence in which the depiction of Marsden undergoes almost no change over eighteen panels. Marsden is being derided by his professors for his poor marks and attendance. "At this rate," a professor tells Jack, "You'll be tugging udders in Kansas. Is that what you want, boy? To be tugging, udders? In Kansas, Jack! For God's sake, Jack, don't let it be udders finally" (5). The first seven unchanging panels mark Marsden's disorientating answer directed at a college professor. With his hands on the desk and a confident smile on his face Jack begins his response. It starts off promising but quickly dissolves into wackiness: "It's not that I haven't got the brains to study, it's that I disagree with it all and can disprove most of it" answers Marsden. He continues:

Sometimes when I look at you, Professor, I see an ignorant gray cancer whose one dubious virtue is that it's technically legal. The teaching professions have perhaps

> **provided an example for the political
> sphere in which sacrifice has been
> redefined as the harm, inconvenience or
> death of others. The universe is self-
> complicating—an atom wants to be a
> germ. But you seem to want to reverse this
> process by means of an ass eclipse. You are
> dry as an Egyptian tomb frog but less pure.
> There's more honest juice in the kernel of a
> spider. Udders aint so bad, Professor. You
> should try 'em some time, if your friends
> will let you. Know the fun. Know the fun.
> Know the fun. (5)**

The strangeness of Marsden's response, however, mimics the illiteracy of authority when faced with honest novelty. The real success here is not that Marsden's rant *does* make sense—because it technically does not—but that it creates the impression of meaninglessness in the face of a conventional righteous retort by a subordinate. The professor is left momentarily speechless and then, through awkwardness, is forced to question to his own peril. The next four panels are without dialogue with Marsden frowning and his hands off the desk (5). This is followed by three close-up versions of the aforementioned panel, three panels with the professor looking inquisitively at Marsden, and the final panel with the baffled professor calling out Marsden's name in an attempt to get the student's attention. The visual skip is then violently brought to an end when Jack stands up and begins firing a gun at two faculty members followed by an entirely meaningless statement: "Stroll on! Toxic darts—the stuff of life! By the time they come around I'll be king of this place and its meager assets! I'm everywhere and in all things and that's fab! Stroll on!" The reader is left asking: is Aylett making a humorous and rather brilliant statement on dismantling the authoritative structure behind fiction— the university is a frequent target of mockery in the comic, after all—and the visual dimensions of comic books by breaking the continuity of meaning and visual progression. Is this amusing episode an act of artistic and semiotic terrorism, or is the scene simply funny because we respond with anxiety to something that eludes our understanding.

There are also recurring tropes in the issue that operate both hypnotically and humorously. The scenes where Sheriff Leonard Bayard is searching for Marsden consistently end with the sheriff musing on the whereabouts of the Caterer: "I wonder what he's doing now?" (3, 7, 10, 25). Each of these musings are followed by inexplicitly bizarre panels that answer what exactly Marsden is doing at that particular moment: showing a girl a snake (3), dancing or perhaps falling backwards (7), holding his friend Gladys hostage (8), wrestling a bird (11), or, as in the final recursion, giving absurd orders to passport control while, in reality, he's standing in a burning building while on the phone with the faculty office.

This recursion is also evident in the narrative and ontological shifts between reality and Marsden's hallucinations; that is, the delusions are consistently terminated by the caption "Back in reality" whereby the narrative returns to reality—which is often as inexplicable as the hallucinatory episodes. It is particularly this relationship between the often meaningless dialogue and peculiar captions that lend the perplexing atmosphere to *The Caterer*.

Aylett's satire intimates a kind of philosophical and aesthetic conviction that phenomenological approaches to comics foster engagement and dynamic readership about the visual medium itself. Etymologically, phenomenology derives from the Greek *phainomenon*, to show, and *logos*, reason or study. So, phenomenological investigation is the study of things shown; from this premise. Aylett's *The Caterer* stresses a visual medium that demonstrates its operations only through active participation. Not only does Aylett want the reader to recognize his or her face in the glass, the project also asks the reader to contemplate the medium itself and its radical possibilities as metonymical of the aesthetic future. Will Eisner famously remarked that comics are sequential art, "the arrangement of pictures or images and words to narrate a story or dramatize an idea" (Eisner 5). Scott McCloud also defines comics with an emphasis on image and sequence: "Juxtaposed pictorial and other images in deliberate sequence, intended to convey information and/or to produce an aesthetic response in the viewer" (McCloud 9). The repetitiveness of Sheriff Bayard's question "I wonder what he's doing now?" becomes absolutely central to the text. Breaking the conventions of conventional storytelling, Aylett places the reader in a position very similar to that of the Sheriff: we expect to follow a sequence of images that will narrate a story but instead we are faced with the dramatization of an affect or an idea. Sequence itself is not safe in *The Caterer* and Aylett discloses its function as a means of making the potentialities of its narrative purpose manifest itself to the reader. Figures 4 and 5 dramatize this kind of unveiling: a sequence of Jack paused and silent, four panels, then three panels, then two panels, each iteration of the panel increasing in its size on the page indicating more anxiety that accompanies the passing of time without content. When interrupted, Jack responds unpredictably and violently; that is, the strangeness of his response demands from the reader a more intense engagement with the narrative and practical possibilities of sequential art.

"Of time it may be said: time times," writes Heidegger in "The Nature of Language,"

> **which means, time makes ripe, makes rise up and grow. Timely is what has come up in the rising. What is it that time times? That which is simultaneous, which is, that which rises up together with its time. And what is that? We have long known it, only we do not think of it in terms of timing. Time times simultaneously: the has-been, presence, and the present that is waiting for our encounter and is normally called the future. Time in its timing removes us into its threefold simultaneity, moves us thence while holding out to us the disclosure of what is in the same time, the concordant oneness of the has-been, presence, and the present waiting the encounter. In removing us and bringing toward us, time moves on its way what simultaneity yields and throws open to it: time-space. But time itself, in the wholeness of its nature, does not move; it rests in stillness. (106)**

Sequence, then, is dimensional and spatial for Aylett. Narrative unfolds in strange ways because, like Jack, time rests in stillness. Its outbursts are not time itself, but the making manifest of a new way of considering narrative: in removing ourselves from our reading we bring ourselves towards ourselves in anxiety and the possibility of thinking what is yet to be thought is thrown open to us. *The Caterer* then heightens our intimation with futurity and, as a result, clearing the possibility for thinking outside bias, tradition, and expectation. The sense of confusion and amusement we get from *The Caterer* is that sense of thinking outside that which we have thought before. So, *The Caterer* may be considered as that which makes us experience angst and anxiety as an analogue to the glass of satire: an intense self-awareness. This awareness, made manifest in such a way that it is *shown* by the comic medium, and the anxiety that accompanies it is what Heidegger identifies as the path to thinking in *What Is Called Thinking?*: the authentic reader "learns when he disposes everything he does so that it answers to whatever essentials are addressed to him at any given moment. We learn to think by giving our mind to what there is to think about" (4). This learning is, as a kind of manifesting the self to the self—radical self-awareness via the radical nothingness that constitutes the self's finitude since, after all, "death is never at stake" (Aylett, *The Complete Accomplice* 308)—made possible through the disposition of anxiety. Aylett's work ultimately provides the *what* there is to think about to which the reader might give his mind: that which has not already been conventionally thought.

In a way, we may consider Aylett's work as didactic, or that which aims to teach its readership *how to see differently* or how we may imagine possibilities. *The Caterer* demonstrates a working analytical approach to this particularly difficult activity: he makes the comic book medium manifest itself as itself. In doing this, Aylett asks readers to negotiate provisional inquiry into thinking in the abyss. By reading Aylett's work one is already internalizing the process and path to thinking. Graphic work forces interpretive instances of anxiety where one must reveal their biases and prejudices to themselves and others in order to proceed with the reading. This intellectual discomfort, however, is made effective via Aylett's brilliant use of humor; the very logic of humor, after all, exposes bias in an analogous way to anxiety. Therefore, the success of this process does not end at critical thinking, but also teaches us how to think critically about critical thinking producing shocking and innovative ways of thinking. So to read Aylett's work is to be challenged, called into question: it is to undergo an experience. Heidegger writes:

> **To undergo an experience with something—be it a thing, a person, or a god—means that this something befalls us, strikes us, comes over us, overwhelms and transforms us. When we talk of "undergoing" an experience, we mean specifically that the experience is not of our own making; to undergo here means that we endure it, suffer it, receive it as it strikes us and submit to it. It is this something itself that comes about, comes to pass, happens. ("Nature" 57)**

In this way, Aylett galvanizes methodological approaches to reading, learning, and thinking. His writing is, in all its pessimism, transformative. So, Aylett's work, with all its scorn, fosters an environment of thoughtfulness, respect, and negotiation: all that which undermines the abuses of authority. The success of Aylett's writing is not necessarily in its confrontational nature but in the way it demands of the reader to submit to thought, to undergo the "relentless onslaught of sheer novelty" (Moore vii), to undergo the transformation that comes to pass, to endure an experience of effortless incitement. The effectiveness of this approach is in its plasticity, in the manner it seeks to unveil and show the processes that underlie our biases. *The Caterer* is effectively that kind of puzzle that is made manifest and notices when it is solved. And once solved something is indeed activated.

Works Cited

Aylett, Steve. *And Your Point Is?: Scorn & Meaning in Jeff Lint's Fiction*. Hyattsville: Raw Dog Screaming Press, 2006.

————. *The Complete Accomplice*. London: Scar Garden Press, 2010.

————. "Jack Marsden Dials I For Inconvenience." *The Caterer #3*. Portland: Floating World Comics, 2008.

————. *Fain The Sorceror*. Hornsea: PS Publishing, 2006.

———— *Lint*. London: Snowbooks, 2007.

Complete Review. "Steve Aylett at The Complete Review." *The Complete Review*. 10 April 2009. Web. 10 Jan. 2016.

Ectric, Bill. "Interview with Steve Aylett." *Literary Kicks*. 25 May 2006. Web. 7 Feb. 2016.

———. "Inside the Head of D. Harlan Wilson." *BillEctric.com*. 12 Sep/ 2011. Web. 7 Feb. 2016.

Eisner, Will. *Comics & Sequential Art*. Tamarac: Poorhouse P., 2005. Print.

Freud, Sigmund. *The Joke and Its Relation to the Unconscious*. Trans. Joyce Crick. New York: Penguin, 2002. Print.

Heidegger, Martin. "The Nature of Language." *On the Way to Language*. Trans. Peter D. Hertz. New York: HarperOne, 1982. 57-108.

———. *What Is Called Thinking?* Trans. J. Glenn Gray. New York: Harper Perennial, 2004. Print.

McCloud, Scott. *Understanding Comics: The Invisible Art*. New York: Harper Perennial, 1994. Print.

Miller, Paul D., aka DJ Spooky that Subliminal Kid. *Rhythm Science*. Cambridge: MIT P, 2004.

Moore, Alan. "Introduction." *Fain the Sorcerer*. Hornsea: PS Pub., 2006. v-viii.

Moorcock, Michael. "Review: *The Velocity Gospel*." *The Guardian*. 10 April 2009. Web. 7 Feb. 2016.

Morrison, Grant. "Review: *Shamanspace*." 10 April 2009. Web. 7 Feb. 2016.

Stone, Jon R. *The Routledge Dictionary of Latin Quotations: The Illiterati's Guide to Latin Maxims, Mottoes, Proverbs and Sayings.* Ed. Jon R. Stone. New York: Routledge, 2005.

Swift, Jonathan. *Jonathan Swift: The Essential Writings: Authoritative Texts, Contexts, Criticism.* Ed. Claude Rawon and Ian Higgins. New York: W. W. Norton, 2010.

Endnotes

[1] See Miller's *Rhythm Science* (2004). See also *Sound Unbound: Sampling Digital Music and Culture* (2008) ed. Paul D. Miller.

[2] See Noon's "Post Futurism Manifesto" (2001), *Cobralingus* (2001), and "The Ghost on the B-Side" (2012).

Goodbye, Beerlight

D. Harlan Wilson

Novahead is the fourth novel in Steve Aylett's Beerlight series alongside *The Crime Studio* (1994), *Atom* (2000) and *Slaughtermatic* (1997) as well as select stories from the fiction collections *Toxicology* (1999) and *Smithereens* (2010). All are stand-alone narratives set in the dystopian, über-absurdist Beerlight City, although *Novahead* features the same protagonist as *Atom*, an unhinged private investigator with a penchant for creative ultraviolence and anabolic proverbs. On the front cover, Alan Moore calls Aylett "[t]he most original and most consciousness-altering living writer in the English language, not to mention one of the funniest." By definition, book blurbs are hyperbolic marketing ploys, but in this case, Moore isn't far off target. A fanatical satirist and provocateur, Aylett writes in multiple genres, often simultaneously, combining elements of science fiction and fantasy with high comedy ("splattershtick") and a high literary aesthetic. As a result of his unique method of hybridization, Aylett's devotees tend to worship him like a bogie in the sky. He's too clever and grandiloquent for genre readers, and he's too *genre* for literary readers, infusing his metanarratives with intricate networks of hi-tech and/or bizarre novums. As a stylist and storyteller, Aylett operates on a plateau that looms in the distance, ahead of his time, and *Novahead* achieves new heights of ingenuity, aesthetics and entertainment. Evidently it will be the last Beerlight novel according to the book description on the back cover. It is a fitting swan song to a series that, at the very least, artfully satirizes the technological pathology of the human condition as seen in real life, American media, and the history of the science fiction genre.

Like *Atom*, the plot of *Novahead* centers on the exploits of "fake detective" Taffy Atom, a riff on the mythological trickster interpellated by outré-noir urbanity. The first sentence sets the tone for the plot's unfolding: "I'd just flicked a spider off the desk, sighed and prepared to rise when the shadow of someone's head and shoulders appeared on the floor like the edge of a jigsaw piece" (9). Immediately the protagonist is confronted by a mysterious figure identified only by its shadow, and a jigsaw-shaped shadow to boot, fore*shadowing* the puzzle that Atom will struggle to put together from beginning to end. (Given Aylett's egregious playfulness with language, this puzzle is as much linguistic as it is narrational). A gunfight and a car chase ensues—the first of many fights and chases, all of them seemingly facilitated by the city itself, a matrix for the nightmare of life: "Buildings the colour of dried blood under a formaldehyde sky. The city and its sundered justifications moved by like a dream. Rain hammering the chassis. Here and there were crushed cars apparently sucked into the asphalt. What doesn't kill you leaves you exhausted" (15). The passage reminisces the famed first line of Gibson's *Neuromancer* (1984), "The sky above the port was the color of television, tuned to a dead channel," emphasizing the lurid, apocalyptic state of the morally and architecturally degraded Beerlight. Aylett and Gibson have much in common, particularly in terms of neologistic density of prose and the degree to which

D. Harlan Wilson

they represent terminal identity. Gibson's method, however, is serious, "realistic" and structurally formulaic, whereas Aylett breaks the rules of causality and (marketable) storytelling at every turn.

As a matter of course, if not orthodoxy, language and ideas take precedence over story in Aylett's work. This is not to say that story doesn't exist; it is merely perfunctory. *Novahead* sees Atom take on the case of a boy with a bomb (i.e., a "nitrophage nerve mine") in his head (hence the title) and he doesn't know what the trigger is. In an effort to find the trigger and save the boy, Atom plumbs the depths of Beerlight, following one lead after another, and dodging death with the eloquence of a drunken Hollywood action-hero who fires guns in tandem with one-liners. This is the plot device - which is to say, *the plot is the device* that allows Aylett to illustrate his uniquely technologized, irreal and parodic urban environment. In so doing, he plays with the conventions of the science fiction genre and, more than anything, ecstatically derides the social, cultural and actual violence that distinguishes America in both the media and real life. While overtly idiosyncratic, Beerlight is a quintessential American city. As Atom explains to one of his many antagonists, Junco, who shoots him point-blank yet fails to produce a bullet hole: "I'm American. . . I breathe through a bullethole."

Virtually all of the characters Atom encounters are eccentric and quirky beyond repair. And that's the point: everybody has been wrecked by Beerlight's fanatic culture machine, which ensures that, "[f]or the average person, there [is] no way to die that [is] not dangerous, inconvenient, or both" (p. 18). Emblematic of this condition is the physically and emotionally Falstaffian Chief Blince, "the man primarily responsible for depicting law enforcement in Beerlight city.

109

Seniority by sheer biomass. His philosophy was the most complete fossil of its kind ever found. I could have sworn I saw a gravitational tide around him, the hidden physics of hypocrisy, its sickly scaffolding shoring up his bulk" (39). Every time Blince enters the page is an opportunity for Aylett to lampoon the stereotype of the meat-headed, donut-eating, alpha-masculine American cop; in one scene, the chief eats a submarine sandwich while engaged in a shootout. Another character, barman Don Toto, is described as perfectly normal yet perfectly broken: "Toto was a bald fellow with all the usual eyes and noses assigned where they might do the least harm. But Toto was smart, a researcher. He had discovered a crime between assault and grievous injury and taken out a copyright. Today most of his body was taped over with bandages. He could barely walk and perhaps didn't want to" (p. 16). There is also Atom, of course, who, according to his poop sheet, "fits the four-point profile for a total bastard. . . . For a while he settled on a campaign of chakric sarcasm using a sleuth cover. . . . His mere face at the window not uncommonly leads to mayhem. . . . So many moral and stylistic ambiguities. He seems to have spent his life stockpiling idiocies for us to scrutinize. Cuffing him'd be like putting a padlock on jello" (52, 53). Like Blince, Toto and Atom, all of Aylett's characters exist somewhere between reality and caricature, usually leaning heavily towards the latter. In essence, they reflect Beerlight's hyperreal landscape, a farcical Baudrillardian Disneyland that signifies the death of reality, the implosion of meaning, and the triumph of American media culture.

Among the most idiosyncratic characters in the city is the city itself, which has as much if not more "personality" than a human being and is *characterized* by the pathology of "gun-lust" that informs the desires of its inhabitants (p. 139). Consider this brief portrayal: "I watched the jagged distance of the skyline, the pinlight of guns firing like synapses across the city surface. A murder of squad cars was parked below, rooflights pulsing . . . They say a city is the detritus left over from a billion scams, but this was a city like broken bones, built too fast and dirty to be intentional" (50, 55). Here and elsewhere, Beerlight emerges as a kind of surging, electric brain distinguished by chronic violence, i.e., the city (a confining and controlling mechanism) facilitates aggression in the bodies and minds of its subjects. Generally speaking, this is a rather prosaic metropolitan function that reminisces Georg Simmel's seminal essay "The Metropolis and Mental Life" (1903). Simmel argues that cities put individuality in jeopardy via the excess of external sensory stimuli that subjects are exposed to. The result is a pathologization of subjectivity that manifests in different ways, some subtle and innocuous, others palpable and destructive. Beerlight's subjects, figurative tentacles of a deranged squid, certainly suffer from this affliction. What distinguishes them is the highfalutin, irreal "temperament" of the urban matrix that produces and manipulates them. Beerlight is at once a city and an un-city, a person and an anti-person.

Perhaps the most colorful and rounded characters in *Novahead*—and most of the Beerlight novels—are guns, the facilities of which are as various as they are innovative, science fictionalized, and patently absurd. Representative examples include the Bohr gun, a "quantum entanglement" weapon that uses "particles of the loaded bullet to activate those of its entangled partner in the victim. The loaded bullet was ejected after operation, as re-firing would only re-install the same quantum bullet in the same impact position" (35-36); the Permutation gun, "which in an instant runs the victim's consciousness through every life state with the intelligence to collate its summation, as a result of which its victim chooses death" (61); the Pound gun, featuring a "pulse grid [that] mapped the room and propelled every local unfixed object after the bullet"; and the Fibonacci pistol, a problematic device in that "once it starts firing it never stops" (131). Described with an overt air of jouissance, guns operate as the definitive markers of identity and dynamic technological extensions of selfhood while maintaining identities and selfhoods of their own; after all, they have extensions, too, bullets, which themselves are equated with living organisms, or at least a human illness: "Bullets have all the qualities of hysteria, Mr Atom—they're fast, go where they're pointed, and travel in herds" (76).

Given the fantastical dynamism of guns, some characters regard them as godlike artifacts, or mediums through which a sort of (ironic) Buddhist enlightenment might be achieved, especially characters like Brute Parker, a "gun saint" who "had always viewed the creation of firearms as a mode of movement toward god" (143). As Atom recounts in a history of the evolution of guns: "For centuries guns merely had a kind of muscle memory, but when fire-by-wire joined the long list of 'self-correcting' systems ripe for disaster, they grew up and filled out. Soon firearms were developing so fast that prototype ammo would arrive old-fashioned in even a point-blank victim. Built-in judgment led to sentience and one night the first gun stole itself" (143). Despite a fierce self-conscious absurdity, one that always already informs his narration, Aylett points to a distinct technoviolent desire, reveling in gunplay while establishing a critique of gunplay as it has been *played out* in American media and reality. Thus he establishes his own *literary* style of gunplay. For me, the issue invokes Cronenberg's *Videodrome* (1983) in which protagonist Max Renn's hand organically fuses with a gun, which ceases to be an extension and becomes part of his core body. By way of this fusion, Renn merges with the gun, and vice versa. In the wake of a killing spree that culminates in suicide, he obtains (potentially) the "new flesh," a state of enlightenment accomplished in the oblivion of video technology. *Novahead* differs considerably from *Videodrome* in scope and tone. Nevertheless guns—and the havoc they wreak, and the physical and ontological carnage they produce—promise characters like Parker a transcendence predicated on ultraviolence. In the alternate (ir)reality of Beerlight, humans and guns, bullets and cities are all mechanisms of ultraviolence that facilitate one another's mania.

If *Novahead* had a thesis, it might be this statement uttered by Toto: "Violence longs to be repeated merely—somehow it's never bored" (67). This is precisely what Aylett's novel does, showing not only how violence is never bored, but never *boring*. He stylizes violence and renders it an art form in terms of the images he depicts, the ideas he conjures, and the melodically pyrotechnic language he uses to express those images and ideas. An expert metanarrationaist, Aylett is ultimately a writer's writer. *Novahead* never only tells a story; it thinks its way through the telling of a story, assessing its own machinery as well as the science fictional machinery (namely cyberpunk) it borrows from and builds upon, and the American machinery it simultaneously lionizes and denigrates. And so, like its various components, all of which seem to be figuratively or literally alive—the book, too, is a sentient organism.

Introduction to *The Complete Accomplice*

Michael Moorcock

For me, there is only one outstanding living English absurdist, in the great tradition of Sterne, Firbank, Richardson or William Burroughs, and that's Steve Aylett. He sees the world in those same strangely consistent terms and, needless to say, doesn't take its pretensions and ambitions hugely seriously. Some of Aylett's funniest work can be found in these wonderful Accomplice novels, which are at last back in print, demonstrating his magnificent talent, his extraordinary imagination and precise, original prose.

When I came across Aylett's work I was genuinely disappointed, filled with regret that I no longer had a magazine in which to publish and publicize him and his work. It isn't every day I have this feeling. Too often the books I see are what I generally call "xeroxes"— effectively copies of copies of copies of other people's novels. It doesn't matter which genre the writers have chosen, whether western, romance, science fiction or "literary," their books offer a thoroughgoing sense of *déjà vu*. Their characters, stories and backgrounds have a familiarity about them that is matched by their over-familiar prose styles. Not so with Aylett, whose freshness and originality I welcomed with delight and considerable relief. His talent continues to exhilarate me and I look forward to his work as I anticipate few others. The Accomplice sequence, in particular, holds a special place in my affections.

In these novels Aylett is at his ebullient, inventive best, his talent concentrated and expansive at the same time. If that seems contradictory, it's because I'm talking about his prose on one hand and his ideas on the other. It was a joy for me to come upon a writer with a style so distinctive and whose ideas are so exuberantly fresh. I found him a joy and set about buttonholing the world and telling it to read him. This was how I felt when I first read *The Eccentricities of Cardinal Pirelli* or *Titus Groan*, the difference being that, unlike Firbank or Peake, when I read them, Aylett was near the beginning of his career and I could (and do) look forward to many more books by him.

Everything about Aylett was fresh. Even the map at the beginning of the first Accomplice book *Only An Alligator* promised something different. From the Awkward Forest down to the Juice Museum everything about it spoke of an author who had abandoned genre altogether, having parodied and lampooned hardboiled detective stories and science fiction hilariously in earlier work like *Slaughtermatic* and *Atom*. My kind of author, in fact, who, after showing what he could do with genre and won his authority, produced work which, like Ballard's or Peake's, was immediately identifiable as that of an idiosyncratic, highly individual writer who took almost nothing seriously except his craft. He had become, if you like, his own genre.

I suppose if Accomplice resembles any genre at all it is closer to the horror story, since the city has humans above and demons below and the two interact, but it is like no horror story you have ever read before and unlikely to appeal to the average *Buffy* or *Elm Street* fan. Although the demons and their deeds are hugely inventive and often pretty grisly, their effect is essentially comic rather than terrifying, the creation of a genuinely fresh imagination as are Aylett's characters – Barny, Sweeney, Gregor and the rest, all of whom would be eligible to join Maurice Richardson's Surrealist Sporting Club (cf *The Exploits of Engelbrecht*) or perhaps hang out with Pere Ubu or even some of the great Boris Vian's characters from *I Spit on Your Graves* or *Heartsnatcher*. Probably Vian, that master of French absurdism, who read science fiction and noir detective novels, played the jazz trumpet and died of a heart attack when watching a movie of one of his books, is the closest comparison we can make, for Aylett has a similarly sardonic view, an unwillingness to compromise at any level, a steady trust in his own strange vision of our world (if it is our world) and its inhabitants, a sardonic inability to force that vision into any mold other than the one he has invented for himself.

Aylett is alone amongst the published writers of his generation in maintaining a steady integrity, refusing compromise and earning the respect of his readers through his persistent consistency, his refusal to meet anyone halfway. He is the kind of writer who, having earned that respect, will continue steadily to gather readers through his career. Those readers, if they are anything like me, will use their enjoyment of books like the Accomplice sequence to determine who they are likely to get on with, just as readers of my generation used the older writers I've mentioned here to decide if they would get on with new acquaintances. That readership is never going to run into massive figures because his books are the very opposite of the crass best sellers we so frequently see in the lists. But it is a discerning, slow-growing readership which, once it has read and enjoyed Aylett, is never going to desert him. I hope I'm addressing that kind of reader here. If I am, I can assure you that you're going to enjoy the ride and that you have much, much more to look forward to. You might find you'll want to do what I usually do, which is to finish the sequence and go straight back to the beginning to read them over again. But whether you're a regular Aylett fan or a new one, I guarantee you'll find nothing quite like this anywhere else in contemporary fiction. Enjoy!

Steve Aylett's *Complete Accomplice* is Not Sane

Sam Reader

"Walking out with the awkwardness of a rod-puppet, he felt like a man leaving a bank with a bar of gold in his pants."

It's already well-documented that I'm a fan of Steve Aylett. *Slaughtermatic* is a fun deconstruction of the cyberpunk genre where the crime actually undoes the plot instead of the reaction to the crime, *Lint* is one of my favorite books of all time, and the other works of his I've read range from merely okay to mind-blowingly fantastic. And then there's *The Complete Accomplice*. Oh, god, there's *Accomplice*. I actually found this when looking for an image to put up for the *Lint* review and ordered it with some birthday money from Amazon. So far, about halfway through, I am not quite disappointed, but I *am* sure that I won't be able to recommend this to anyone. Also, I'm positive that *Lint* was Aylett's response to critics of *Accomplice*, a sort of twisted self-parody with an expy of himself as the lead. *The Complete Accomplice* is not a sane book. It does not work in sane circles, nor should it. *Accomplice* is, in fact, so gibberingly mad that it pretty much guarantees its own hilarity, provided you're accepting enough of its madness. I understand this will not be for everyone. I understand that many may not find this book humorous, or assume it is just being (*shudder*) "weird for weirdness's sake" or something equally as shrill and odious. However! This is a brilliant book, an almost completely successful attempt to write something new. Whether it succeeds or not is up for grabs, but hell, at least it tries to go all the way, instead of sticking in "safe" waters like every other book of its type. While that can be said of most Bizarro Fiction, Aylett's manner of making everything so commonplace and non-threatening even in the most grotesque of circumstances gives him an edge that many of the others in his field don't have. And it works, in its own unsettling, twisted way.

The Complete Accomplice (2010) is a collection of four novels that were originally published separately: *Only An Alligator* (2001), *The Velocity Gospel* (2002), *Dummyland* (2003), and *Karloff's Circus* (2004) that feature mostly the same characters in a city called Accomplice.

Only an Alligator tells the story of Barny Juno, a mild-mannered animal collector who is of no threat to anyone. One day, while going through a "creepchannel", a sort of shortcut that heads through the kingdom of demons beneath the island city of Accomplice, Barny finds an alligator. Completely ignorant to the fact that picking up reptiles from ethereal channels to netherworldly areas is a bad thing, Barny names the alligator "Mr. Newton" and takes it to his house, which doubles as an animal sanctuary containing mascara-wearing dogs and a fluctuating number of eels. What he doesn't know is that his "rescue" of the alligator has deprived the King of Demons, a large white cockroach named Sweeney, of a very important meal - the alligator has picked up all kinds of information, and was destined to be Sweeney's dinner until it was stolen. Sweeney launches a campaign of blackmail and assassination (both character and otherwise) to bring Barny down and recover the alligator before anyone can learn anything from it, utilizing the Mayor's office, and both the incumbent and challenging mayoral candidates. Barny is suddenly the target of a great deal of demonic attention, smear campaigns, and other equally ludicrous events, all of which he is completely oblivious to and tries tirelessly to ignore when he can notice them.

That I was able to type the last paragraph with a straight face and absolutely no hint of irony or "what the hell did I just write?" is a testament to *Accomplice's* power, but it's more than just insane set pieces and crazy names. The last sentence is completely accurate - Barny has no idea he's been targeted by demons until the last third of the book, and proceeds mainly to ignore most of the attention directed his way. The machinations fail completely without his input one way or the other. This makes it unique in another way - usually, the hero would be either directly responsible, or there would be a team of people around him, fighting to keep things ordinary. Instead, the only one who realizes anything is going on is Barny's best friend, Edgy. And when he reveals that demons are after Barny for his alligator (shortly after punching out all of King Sweeney's teeth in a vicious beatdown that comes almost out of nowhere), no one really cares. They go back to arguing about dinner and the alligator is eventually dealt with in the most innocuous way possible.

Which is not to say that any of it is boring. Aylett's vivid imagination keeps it far from that, be it the odd traditions of the city of Accomplice, or the massive and expensive smear campaign against a complete nobody who has no idea what's going on.

The book is also gruesomely violent, from the opening that talks of Sweeney dragging a philosopher down to the netherworld and eating his brains while he continues to spout nonsense, to Edgy's back-alley brawl, to Barny's unsettling habit of eating baby trolls when he gets nervous. The characters all feel like real people and real friends, too - they have their own nicknames for each other, help each other with ridiculous schemes, and have long, protracted dinners and conversations with each other. You could know these people, if their circumstances weren't so ridiculously twisted by the place they live in.

At the same time, though, they're just as insane as their circumstances. GI Bill, one of the characters, spends his time engaged in a blood feud with Barny's sidekick Gregor over Gregor being stuck in a dinosaur during a ball game. Sweeney uses all his influence to smack around a person who doesn't even care if he exists. The challenger to the incumbent mayor is referred to as "doomed Eddie Gallo" and has to give speeches in a torture device. That Aylett makes this relatable and amusing helps push the book over the edge for me. You come to accept what *Accomplice* throws at you, and unlike Kris Saknussemm's *Private Midnight*, it doesn't do it to shock you all the more, it does it so you can understand the motivations of the characters and the plots that wind up in play. It does it so you can get Accomplice and all its myriad nuttiness.

The book is not without its bad points. The plot is heavily involved and dense, but completely inconsequential in places. It is filled with bizarre turns of phrase, irrational characters, and Aylett handles everything with the same nonchalance. Overall, the book is barely comprehensible at best.

But in the end, it's fascinating, though inaccessible. The set pieces are hilarious, and the strange syntax makes even the smallest and most inconsequential sentence suddenly very descriptive. While I can't recommend it to anyone in particular (okay, if you liked Lint, you can probably attempt Accomplice with a degree of ease), it's an essential book to me, one that should be read and, in an era of imitations, possibly be followed to help make something new, something more interesting. Read this book. It'll twist your head into all kinds of interesting shapes and hopefully make you laugh at the same time.

For the most part, my impressions of *Accomplice* remain unchanged. In the final two books, it's still as barely-coherent, insane, and darkly hilarious as the first two. The characters, while they become more aware of the situation going on, still remain just as odd and yet somehow compelling, Barny still remains almost as much out of his depth (the final book has him willingly going into something called a "blood shed" and giving his blood willingly for a levy) and accepting of his circumstances, and overall not much changes. Though that might actually be the point.

You see, I'm beginning to get the sense that *Accomplice* is actually a version of *The Divine Comedy* where no one notices what's going on, or even cares. The secret underground cadre of demons would suggest that Accomplice is some level of hell, as well as things like the Blood Clock in the center of the city, the rather gruesome levy (and there's the chance that some people with that levy *might be giving too much,* as seen in the final chapters of book four), and the massive barbed-wire sculpture the incumbent mayor's challenger (the mayor being someone who not only acquiesces to the demons, but also serves their wishes) has to give his speeches in. But despite all the insanity and the nightmarish visuals (the Church of Automata in particular fills me with nonspecific dread), you will still find the heroes dining at the Ultimatum Restaurant or preparing for a picnic in the Infernal Realms. Adding to this mess is the list of questions in the back that reference angels, demons, and "people outside Accomplice" that seem to place it as either a hell similar to *Jacob's Ladder*, or some kind of purgatory. Barny's apparent ascension to a higher state at the end of book four merely adds credence to this assumption. Of course, then the reasoning would lead us to believe that all of these people haven't been particularly good but need to be redeemed somehow. The mechanic, Mike, and Barny would be the prime examples of this - both of them wind up being redeemed . . . Mike turns into an angel, sort of , and Barny ascends to the point that even after he implodes due to an over-levy, he is still seen and interacts with the other characters, even providing references for jobs they get (meaning that he can still influence Accomplice). Still, the idea that humans set up their own society regardless of the purgatory brewing beneath is a great one, and *Accomplice* still ranks highly in terms of original ideas

The other thing of note is that the book gets more sinister as it goes along, adhering more to Saknussemm's Progression. For those of you who follow me regularly, Saknussemm's Progression is the process that Kris Saknussemm perfected in which ideas get progressively weirder and the reader gets bombarded by them to the point that they become commonplace, and then weirder, more menacing ideas arc introduced so the reader gets even more freaked out. *Accomplice is* actually doing this, though it doesn't start ramping up until the last two books. While initially it hadn't done this and seemed to be avoiding this kind of thing, it does it simply to change the mood - yes, everything is still satirical and laughable, but with an increasingly sinister edge. That sinister edge is what changes it. While it's comic fantasy, it makes it more and more difficult to laugh at it, and the environment becomes more and more alien.

While the world of *Accomplice* wasn't really that much like ours to begin with, as the demons begin to meddle more and more, it becomes a stranger place, a less hospitable sort of crazy and a more dangerous kind. While before Sweeney still dragged people to hell, it seemed to be played for laughs. Things like the Levy, the Church of Automata, and the like are frightening and sinister, but don't seem to be particularly threatening. As it comes together, it becomes funny much in the way of a darkly comic funhouse - frightening, but somehow so absurd that you continue laughing at it. I have to admit, this is a manner of dark comedy that actually seems to work, neither light enough to be mistaken for straight comedy, nor so dark that it could actually pass for a horror novel.

In conclusion, *The Complete Accomplice* is still everything I thought it would be. Dark, hilarious, freaky, unsettling, weird, and all together enjoyable. Can I recommend it to anyone? If you liked what I put forward in these reviews, then maybe I can.

On the Philosophical Narratology of Steve Aylett's *Shamanspace*

Iain Matheson

0. Introduction

Examining *Shamanspace's* first two chapters, one can discover a bit of philosophy available to exhumers of diegetic Being; a bit of philosophy incongruous with the expressed philosophy of one of the characters, posing a problem for Aylett scholars.

The essay that follows will enact such an examination. In the first section, I shall pass through logic and structuralism to arrive at a (narratological) concept of story. In the second section, I shall use that concept to put chapters 1-9 in diegetic, and - thereby - a philosophical, context. As I do so, the above-named bit of philosophy will emerge. In the third section, I shall present the problem thereby posed to Aylett scholarship, and conclude with a nod to the critical future.

1. Needful Things

I shall begin with an operational definition.

Take a non-minimal, fictive prose narrative, - novel, novella, novelette, or short story (cf. "FAQ.") - and express its action after the formula "$((((A \wedge B) \wedge C) \wedge D) \wedge E) ....$"[1] Compose your expression such that

> the action-sentences are in chronological order,

and

> none overlaps any other at the level of a condition sufficient for truth.[2,3]

Assuming that you have been successful, you will have made an expression, the logical form of which is a consistent bi-lateral proposition; one, the necessary and sufficient condition of whose truth is the truth of both of its - simpler - sides, or conjuncts.[4]

In other words, you will have made a consistent expression, the truth of which would indicate the truth of either of its conjuncts: one, the truth of which would be logically posterior to the truth of each of its conjuncts: *one, the truth of which would logically depend on the truth of each of its conjuncts.*

Now, in this essay, I assume a truth-conditional semantics: a theory, such that

> the *meaning* of a sentence is to be sought in the set of conditions that *would* suffice for its (that sentence's) truth, and

> the *sense* of a sentence, if any, is to be sought in the condition that *does* suffice for its truth.

This semantics granted, your expression will present some arresting properties. Provided it be true, one (and only one) of the conditions sufficient for its truth will have been actualised; - thus one (and only one) of the conditions sufficient for the truth of each conjunct will have been actualised - and your expression will have taken on one (and only one) sense; - thus each conjunct will have taken on one (and only one) sense - what is more, the conjunction's sense will incorporate that of each conjunct; finally, neither conjunct's sense will be able to die from the death of the other's. Àpropos of the last point, we must say something similar of your action-sentences: of none will the sense be able to die from the death of any comparable sense(s), for the meaning of none of your action-sentences will share anything with the meaning of any (of the) other(s).

Still assuming it to be true, then, your statement will shock in two ways – (linguistic and narratological.

a.   Linguistic.

Your expression will be non-lingual.

The sufficing truth-condition of the right-, will matter to the left-, hand conjunct in one connection at most, whether you substitute the right-hand conjunct with any - available - conjunct; thus the - situational - sense of the right-hand conjunct will have an aspect unalterable by substituting its (that conjunct's) stuff with the stuff of any other (available) conjunct.[5] In one of its aspects, then, the (situational) sense of the right-hand conjunct will be unconditional on certain differences: it will be trans-, or non-, structural, i.e., - for the known human purposes - non-lingual. (Cf.

Derrida 278-80, 292.) *The expression of which it is a part, of course, will also be non-lingual.*

b. Narratological.

Your action-sentences' referents will be causally disconnected; otherwise, some such referent(s) would be logically posterior to (an)other(s), - the sufficient truth-condition of some action-sentence(s) would be logically posterior to the sufficient truth-condition of (an)other(s) - which would violate the logical form of your expression.

We are ready, now, to mark a crucial equivalence.

Still assuming it to be true, your expression will - let us say – "'name'" what the narratologist Manfred Jahn would recognise as your narrative's *story;* it will "'name'" 'the chronological sequence of events,' without 'logical' or - therefore – 'causal structure' (Jahn). More than this, no expression of a different logical species will do as much.[6] *It follows that your expression will be of the same logical species as any (Jahnian) story.*

It remains to remark that every diegesis is, - after its fashion - i.e., that your expression *will* be true; it also remains to remark that, every (true) story boiling down to a logically comparable expression, no story*telling* will be lingual.

We can proceed to *Shamanspace.*

2. *Shamanspace,* at last

In the chapter before chapter 1, Sig - a member of a faction of wannabe god-killers, known as the Internecine - is taken by Melody, his better, to visit the soul-scarred Alix, one of the faction's failed deicides. Sig asks Alix about his (Alix's) one, abortive attempt on god, whereupon

> **sudden pockets of failure went geomantic, flashed into expression, twisting the moment through the room. He [Alix] had abruptly opened his pain. Sig saw Alix journeying in the big huge, an electron speck on electric white.**
>
> **"Yeah, it's a little bit triggery," said Alix. "I mean it. Into every word I weave thorns." (Aylett 18)**

There, the chapter closes. Chapter 1 opens:

> **The girl was surgeon and singing bird, deadly queen of sharps. Resentments at the ready, we met in a nerve storm club. (Aylett 21)**

There is much in these lines to unpack.

The pockets' going geomantic *hangs with* their flashing into expression; witness the parataxis of "went [...], flashed." The moment is twisted through the room *in consequence of* this going, this flashing; witness the present continuous "twisting" after "expression." The same twisting *follows* Alix's opening his pain; witness the past perfect "he had [...] opened." Alix calls what Sig beholds "a little bit triggery;" witness the referents open to the relevant "it." (Barring a new antecedent, then, the next "it"" Alix uses unbound by a propositional attitude will refer to what Sig beholds: what Sig beholds is - publicly - *the thing* on Alix's tongue.) A moment later, Alix repeats his claim; his "I mean ..." binds "that it's a little bit triggery," and - so - is disquotable. Finally, Alix speaks of "every word," i.e., essays a universal statement; at the same time, he specifies no domain. (Every word of what character?) Still, the phrase has significance straightaway; he means "every word of what you, Sig, behold."[7] - What Sig beholds, then, *signifies*. - Alix finishes by explaining that "every word['s] [... being] thorn"y generates the "trigger" attribute in what Sig beholds. (To test this, substitute for "Into every word I weave thorns," a sentence that names no state of affairs readily sufficing for such a triggeriness - e.g.: "For a long time, I retired early." Something should feel different in the *meaning* of Alix's remarks.)

We can use all this - and move forward in our work - answering two questions: what words are involved in what Sig beholds? and what is in "the moment [that twists] through the room?"

a. What words are involved in what Sig beholds?

In the chapter before chapter 1, Sig encourages Alix to "remember' finding god's heart" (Aylett 17); Alix opens his pain; - that signal of his past - finally, a geomantic moment twists through the room, and Sig beholds - thorny, i.e. triggery - words, and sees Alix, journeying. In other words, asked to remember his abortive deicide, Alix offers the history of his injury; geomancy follows, and Sig beholds words, and sees Alix, journeying. To put it differently, Sig receives words geomantically from Alix; words that tell Alix's coming to be scarred.

Now, chapters 1-9 tell the same tale. It follows that the words involved in what Sig beholds, and the words of chapters 1-9, share, not only a story, but a *lingual* function: neither Sig's, nor the chapters', words will be "'those'" of a story. In addition, both Sig's, and the chapters', words might be called thorny: triggery: they are, in a similar way. In sum, the words involved in what Sig beholds, and the words of chapters 1-9, do one thing, - a thing that exceeds, though indicating, a shared "'storytelling'" - and they do it in something approaching one way: sharing unapproachable depths, they are also - perhaps arbitrarily - similar. Put differently, *the words involved in what Sig beholds are a variation on - are, perhaps, one with - those of chapters 1-9.*

b. What is in "the moment [that twists] through the room?"

Sig's seeing Alix, journeying, is indicated by his (Sig's) participating in geomancy, i.e., by his participating in divination from ground or land.[8] *At the same time,* Sig's seeing Alix, journeying, is indicated by his consuming certain words, to wit, those of chapters 1-9.

Now, sufficient conditions are not co-actualisable; it follows that Sig's participating in geomancy *is* his consuming the words of chapters 1-9.

In other words, in "the moment [that twists] through the room," we find a production of (some variation on) chapters 1-9.

We are ready, now, to put that production in "diegetic, and - thereby - a philosophical, context."

2.2 To Philosophy ...

We may say of any narrative that it generates - indicates - a story. If that narrative targets - or decides - that-A,[2] then that-A will be folded into said story. (Conversely, if that-A is never folded into the story, then the narrative will neither have targeted, nor have decided, that-A.) In addition, if the narrative neither targets, nor decides, that-A, then that-A will not be folded into the story.

The story, of course, will amount to a - partial - inventory of the - relevant - diegesis: every act/event it (that story) "'targets'" will have been put into - or effected by (part of) - said diegesis; such acts and/or events as it does not, will not, i.e., will have no diegetic existence.

Now, as of chapter 1, we must say that the production divined by Sig succeeds its divination, i.e., occurs within certain - temporal - boundaries; however, the narrative has neither stated, nor given it to be decided, just when it (that production) occurs. - *Neither that it occurred at such-and-such a time, nor that it didn't, has been targeted/decided: that it occurred at {any given time} has been left both unstated and undecidable.* - In consequence, if *Shamanspace* ended a line into chapter 1, then (the event of) Sig's production would be folded into the story, but without a - definite - time of occurrence: after a point, it would be spread out like an electron.

What is more, *for all we discover of that production, S h a m a n s p a c e may as well end a line into chapter 1.* Notably, its (said production's) occurrence is never given - and nor is it implied to have - a (definite) time: after a point, that production *will* be spread out in the story like an electron.

What philosophical context does this generate?

Well, since the story "'targets'" Sig's production neither as occurring, nor as failing to occur, at {any given time}, (diegetically,) it (that production) is a-temporal: it is never *with* any character: it never shows itself.

In the chapter before chapter 1, however, Sig has the chance to behold it "from itself in the very way in which it shows itself from itself" (Heidegger 58); - *the chance to exhume its (diegetic) Being* - in other words, he has the chance to behold, *and - so - become able to imagine*, a thing (going) unbeheld: *he has the chance to be, in a perspicuous refutation of Berkeley's "master argument,"* [10,11] or in some redemption of things from god.

Such is the philosophical context in which I wish to put the "production of [...] chapters 1-9" divined by Sig.

The redemption itself, of course, is the "bit of philosophy" anticipated by the Introduction, and the world of *Shamanspace* is haunted by it; but what "problem" does it "pose ... for Aylett scholars?"

3. and Beyond! (Conclusion)

In reply, I note an incongruity. By Being, Sig's production redeems things from god, - in one connection, at least - but it also affords a narrator who insists that "god [...] runs through all matter" (Aylett 32). Should Aylett scholars take this to mean that said production undermines its own narrator? should they treat chapter 9 (Aylett 103) as the tale of an *empathic* identification with god, i.e., as the tale of a non-gnostic union with godhead? the tale of an *Imaginary* opus? Have we, here, a psycho-analysis of certain peak states? Have we, by contrast, a theology of egoism?

I commend these questions to the critical future.

Works Cited

A Dictionary of the Derivations of the English Language. London and Glasgow : William Collins, Sons, & Co. Ltd. 1872. Print.

Aylett, Steve. *Shamanspace.* Brighton: Codex. 2001. Print.

Berkeley, George. *The Works of George Berkeley, DD.* Vol. 1. London : J. F. Dove. 1820. Print.

Derrida, Jacques. *Writing and Difference.* Trans. Alan Bass. London : Routledge. 1997. Print.

"FAQ." *Science Fiction and Fantasy Writers of America.* SFWA, January 2013. Web. 31 December 2013. <http://www.sfwa.org/nebula-awards/nebula-weekend/faq/>

Gallois, A. "Berkeley's Master Argument." *The Philosophical Review 83* (1974): 55–69. Print.

Heidegger, Martin. *Being and Time.* Trans. John Macquarrie and Edward Robinson. Oxford : Blackwell. 2005. Print.

Jahn, Manfred. *Narratology: A Guide to the Theory of Narrative.* Version 1.8. Universität zu Köln, 2005. Web. 1st May 2016. http://www.uni-koeln.de/~ame02/pppn.htm

Endnotes

1 Here, '^' reads "and:" the formula is a conjunction. Each letter will stand for a declarative sentence in re: one or more of your narrative's acts and/or events: each will stand for an *action-sentence* drawn on that narrative.

Note: I am - and throughout this essay, will be - using the predicate calculus.

2 Note: the - temporal - order of the action-sentences will not be a sufficient truth-condition of any action-sentence.

3 To achieve non-overlapping, it may not be enough to assign an action-sentence to each act/event; a prose narrative may contain (an) act(s)/event(s) indicating or indicated by (an) other act(s)/event(s). However, having made such an assignment, you *may* find it helpful to follow these instructions:

> Group your sentences as follows.

1. Put sentences overlapping at, or - let's say - sharing, a sufficient truth-condition into a group.

2. Put sentences sharing a sufficient truth-condition with any sentence of that group into that group.

3. Repeat step 2 until no sentence shares a sufficient truth-condition with any sentence of that group.

4. Arrange the sentences in that group in chronological order.

After that,

> assign an action-sentence to each group.

> *Use only these higher-level action-sentences to compose your expression.*

On the Philosophical Narratology of *Shamanspace*

4 C'onsistent?' Yes; (the logical form of) any narrative will be consistent; every narrative selects fictive, from all possible, sentences; inconsistency would preclude - such a - selection, i.e., would preclude narrativity.

5 The available conjuncts will exclude false, as they will meaningless, conjuncts; any conjunct of either of these kinds would destroy, rather than affect, the sense under consideration.

6 N'o expression of a different logical species will do the same?' Well, let the logical species of an expression be the species determined by its logical form. Your expression's logical form will comprise a *consistent conjunction* whose conjuncts *do not overlap at the level of a condition sufficient for truth;* formally, then, an expression of a different logical species will comprise a formula *inconsistent,* and/or *not a conjunction,* and/or one whose conjuncts *do overlap at the level of a condition sufficient for truth.* In case it is inconsistent, such an expression will shadow no narrative; - cf. footnote 5 - in case it is not a conjunction, it will target no sequence; in case its conjuncts overlap, it will support logical structure: in none of these cases will it amount to a (Jahnian) story.

7 *How* the phrase has been completed, I find it harder to say. It (said phrase) appeals to no pro-forms, i.e. amounts neither to anaphora nor to deictic exophora; what is more, it appeals to no defining context, i.e., amounts to no homophora; finally, it occurs in a singular context, - this most enigmatic of dieseses - i.e., can appeal to nothing pragmatic. We may suspect some other exophora; - what Sig beholds is - publicly - on Alix's tongue as he (Alix) speaks - there again, we may suspect that here, English "'is'" figuring one of its own - an-ontological - limits, a certain, vanished semiotics.

8 "Geomancy" derives from the ancient Greek *ge-* (the earth) + *manteia* (divination) (*A Dictionary of the Derivations of the English Language* 160, 247)

9 Note: "A" names a sentence that names (an) act(s) and/or event(s).

10 For this phrase, cf. (Gallois).

138

<u>11</u> Berkeley's "master argument" runs roughly as follows: it being impossible to imagine an unperceived existent without imagining - hence perceiving - it, - it being, then, impossible to imagine an unperceived existent - an unperceived existent cannot be conceived (cf. Berkeley 34); in consequence, each existent is essentially perceived, and god needful for the continuity of existence.

Frisky Skylarking: Political Satire in the Accomplice Quartet

Tony Lee

"If you want to tell people the truth, make them laugh."
—Oscar Wilde

The first book of Steve Aylett's Accomplice series, *Only An Alligator* (Aylett 11-109), depicts political motivations in the midst of chaos, but the familiar is given a corkscrew twist. In the strange township of Accomplice – an anagram of "comic place" – hapless hero Barny Juno works in the post office sorting room, and he runs, quite amateurishly, it must be said, an animal shelter (for monkeys and lions, not donkeys). Basically, he is a placid individual who's undeserving of the "danger man" reputation that delights his friends but, when our protagonist takes his new adopted pet alligator out for walkies, poor Barny is targeted as a malcontent and troublemaker by corrupt Mayor Rudloe.

Perhaps the wilder animals are metaphorical dissidents, as dangerous to the general public and authority figures as they are to friends of their caretaker, if rarely to Barny himself. I greatly enjoyed the set of four original books, but this article quotes from a reading of the collected/revised omnibus edition. What makes *Accomplice* so worth re-reading is

141

the fabulous scenario is open to numerous reinterpretations. Failing - as have most politicians - in his desperate attempts to dramatize the ledger, Rudloe (an anagram of louder) speaks out, as if offering a sarcastic taunt against public protest:

"I have asked you to infest this square in order to impart a warning of a dire threat to our community... but as Accomplice's single organ of government... I must talk to you regarding certain bastards who would defame our imploded society" (Aylett 114).

This merits our attention as foresight about the real world's "Occupy" movement. The Mayor continues, thusly: "I will decide in due course that the levy must be increased to counter the baleful crisis. At that time, I will set upon a policy greatly at odds with your wellbeing" (16) – with a thinly disguised, and predictive, caution that sounds very much like an honest translation of rabidly Tory propaganda, and current Republican rhetoric. After decades of privatization and deregulation, Conservative hypocrisy is what burdens us today, exposed for precise targeting by sundry bullets of witty wisdom in Aylett's prose.

Hiding out among the historical detritus of a local museum during the town's annual Plunder Parade does not answer the Mayor's slanderous campaign against Barny, but does allow for plenty of unbelievably funny situations to ensue, on Accomplice streets where craziness is more important than sanity. Aylett's characters are greater–than–life figures, but his heroes embody many of the maverick traits we all aspire to, while some of the human antagonists are not unlike those annoying relatives that it's often best to avoid. *Only An Alligator* is a fat–free volume of remarkably caustic satire and genre parody with a bundle of one–

liner gags that make acerbic Ben Elton's diatribes seem like Danielle Steel.

PLAYING BINGO TRUMP CARDS

Of particular merit are the random snippets of wisdom from the shrewd philosophy of famous 'brain-saver' Bingo Violaine, quoted by everyone to bolster arguments for their personal views and political agendas. Steve Aylett possesses and demonstrates an impertinent genius for great character names. Bingo Violaine always puts me in mind of the Archimedean (with the accent on comedian!) exclamation 'eureka', and the Enlightenment resource Voltaire. And yet pedants might argue that Aylett's key inspiration was the song "Mr. Bingo" (Verlaine) from ex-Television guitarist Tom Verlaine's first solo album. Even as outrageously mystifying events settle, like Aylett's dust monkeys, around the chapter quotes from Violaine, the freefall narrative of *Only An Alligator* spirals down to Hell, and then flies away at a number of unexpected tangents, going faster and further to wacky and surreal extremes, until a final confrontation between dumbly valiant Barny, the routinely contemptible Rudloe, and those pesky demons.

While some US senators and GOP candidates (of Tea Party ilk) make themselves into worldwide laughingstocks with outrageous comments that expose the depths of their comprehensive ignorance, it almost seems as if Rudloe has predicted, or is somehow influencing (does his contempt for reality know no bounds?), the current malaise of actual global politics. As the mouthpiece of madness in Accomplice, the swaggering Mayor (who shrugs with one shoulder, just like people - in the real world - lean on one elbow) emerges from the debacle as exactly the kind of politician that we love to hate. Funny sketches involving other Accomplice characters comment, sometimes obliquely, on real world political debate and the deplorable lack of basic intelligence or attention in such discussions. Freedom of speech is funny that way.

Repetition of the circular "Snail, Sarge?" (81, 178-79, 243, 344) dialogue in each Accomplice novel does seem rather like someone interviewing a politician - or any other subordinate questioning an authority figure in the approved Kafkaesque manner. We have seen government ministers in blithely evasive performances on TV. In May 1997, the BBC program *Newsnight* saw the farce of then Home Secretary Michael Howard being interviewed by Jeremy Paxman, who asked a specific question repeatedly but received no direct answer (*Newsnight*). By avoiding precise and informative responses, politicians are unwittingly exploring or spreading a bitter sense of Pythonesque absurdity in dialogue and, like hapless characters embracing such a comedy sketch mentality… well, they don't mind if they do.

Battling any function, trickster Prancer Diego is unmatched at useless activity. "He'd dig a hole, do a headstand in it and claim he was wearing the entire world as a hat" (Aylett 125). It is hardly a great stretch of imagination to perceive a critique of Texan cowboy George W. Bush in that larking image. Aylett keenly sums up in a sentence what Oliver Stone attempted in biopic, *W* (2008), about infamous president 'Dubya' . With the advent of the second volume, *The Velocity Gospel*, Diego expresses his support for the Mayor of Accomplice, but remains nonetheless prone to bouts of frivolous anarchy: "Authority – let us do it the supreme honor of incessant disregard" (Aylett 126). He recognizes a truism that "Apologies are tools of control" (146). Oddly enough, Prancer Diego can be anagrammed to 'creep adoring' and, being one of those supporting players that our relatively innocent protagonists – like the puzzled Barny and flustered Gregor – turn to for advice, this is not a good thing.

While touting nonsense products as a doorstep salesman, socially inept Gregor, the Round One, consults the Grand Dollimo at the Church of Automata, and is told: "You echo with dominoes, all those clinking dogmas. You need merely choose one and the noise ends" (129-30). The comfortable certainties of religious belief are reassuring to the lost, but, like playing dominoes, the pattern is formed by only arbitrary connections, and the domino effect lurks like a clichéd prophecy of doomsday. Visiting the Fuseheads at the Powderhouse temple, Gregor seeks further enlightenment and is criticized for his "tentative misdemeanors" (131-32) and "inconvenient fancies" (132), but informed "should we find that you're a real delight, the prospects are practically limitless" (132). It is not just in showbiz that nonentities can prosper; modern politics thrives upon "the glory of the blur" (132), and never mind the weakness of worshipping ultimate weapons. Facing mortal danger, Gregor is promised sweet treats yet dares to ask, "What flavour?" (133). Fusemaster Jayrod chides him: "Do not question your god" (133).

ENEMY OF THE STATUS QUO

Is Rudloe the new Number Two? Although there are no direct equivalents, character–wise, some of the inhabitants of Accomplice, like those of other communities found in many fabled towns in genre fiction, or its related media, are not unlike the archetypes in the Village of Patrick McGoohan's cult classic TV series *The Prisoner* (1967), which also dealt with various political themes, and did so with an astutely sardonic edginess that invites comparison with every new fictional society in genre literature. Perhaps it is too much of a stretch to suppose that Barny is any kind of alter-ego for Number Six in *The Prisoner*, but political and philosophical conflicts in the Accomplice novels are vaguely reminiscent of the clashing ideologies depicted in that show.

Having no luck with attempts to demonize Barny, the scheming Rudloe concocts an entirely fictitious foe to oppose. However, as if to save the Mayor's hidden Janus face, the imaginary Cyril Movement springs into active life in Accomplice, presenting itself as graffiti slogans initiated by a suicidally irrepressible Prancer Diego, causing a rash of embarrassment during the Mayor's election campaign because instead of a miracle, "the most authority [should have] to grapple with is normal human disinterest" (141). This outlandish manifesto is revealed as damaging to Rudloe's prospects of getting in with the Conglomerate. He muses: "There's information in a hoax" (143). But, it is "a tragedy on the street when acid words effect democracy, eh?" (143). Is the Cyril farce attributable to the Mayor's own speechwriter, Noam B. Turbot (quirkily, an anagram of rant mob bout)? Turbot admits his job "is to adapt the presentation of the client's will to the prejudices of the public, so that one is well served and the other feels so for a time" (148). It is a nearly perfect assessment of the fleeting appeal of today's political broadcasting standards.

"Cyril invented concern" (*Accomplice* 150) is the dubious slogan of a concocted enemy movement in the

Mayor's re–election campaign. Rudloe is annoyed by the immediate public success of his phantom counterpart: "Cyril smiles a block away" (156) like the ghost of a revolutionary influence "and obsessional fringe groups are born" (156). Bemusingly, however irreverent it may be, idealism seems harder to destroy, or even oppose, than the people who follow its notions.

While in a Czarist/president-for-life mood, the Mayor contemplates re-naming the residential palace Rudloe Manor, because then, "no-one else will ever preside here" (157). In confessional mode, consulting his traitorous legal advisor and sidekick lackey, Max Gaffer, Rudloe admits, in a curious twist upon celebrity narcissism, "My hair was my conscience, I was glad when it went" (176). There is a listing of Rudloe's speeches, all titled like monologues, including "I Serve You Though You Sicken Me" (216) and "Look At The State Of You" (216), which now sound like Mitt Romney's brand of graceless cynicism. It all adds up to a portrait of demagoguery for Rudloe that's as disquieting as it is hilarious.

Rudloe courts a sinister Conglomerate that proves to be inhuman in its composition, at least in its committee form: "how else could their joint intelligence and morality be less than their individual intelligence and morality?" (157). This chimes with the findings of documentary, *The Corporation* (2003), a film that studies the apparent "personality" traits demonstrated by the corporation - if viewed as a legal body - and concludes that if a corporation was indeed a single person, that individual would be a psychotic. It is a grimly mundane valuation that beds down easily with the distinctively supernatural horrors of a generally macabre underworld kingdom of "Cold Hell" (in the

Accomplice books), ruled by the Lovecraftian monster Sweeney.

When Max visits Sweeney, down below, he formally introduces himself: "Distortion's the game - I pretend it's not a luxury, or that there's such a superabundance of truth that the luxury of distortion is okay for a laugh" (Accomplice 205). This reveals, and revels in, not just the typical mind games of legal proceedings, but the commonplace duplicity and "ulterior nervous system" (205) of many lawyers in literary fiction and media incarnations; insistent upon "the hobbling of humanity" (206). It explains how "The law is a collection of intimidations" (206) that "poses as reality" (206) in court. But there is no truth, only hells open to negotiation. This stands as a grossly cynical attitude that is familiar to us all; whether our knowledge was gleaned from watching numerous TV dramas (from *Boston Legal* to *Damages*), or from bitter first-hand experience of dealing with solicitors - whether, like Max Gaffer, they are precious about their underwear or not.

ANY EXCUSE WILL DO

As a ridicule of oaths of allegiance that award citizenship to immigrants and cultural outsiders, the Powdermouth gospel is more than satisfactorily scathing. Rod Jayrod remarks to Gregor that no bid for velocity can be heard, or accepted, "without a full recital of the Ballistic Catechism" (157) The worried Gregor's blasphemous answers to the Fusemaster's questionnaire result in denying the Round One a blue touch–paper to wear. Don't know enough cultural trivia about your own country? How dare you call yourself British, or American, or..?

At a public meeting of Cyril supporters, Prancer Diego's one brief moment of sanity is able to declare: "Fascism is born of the idea that progress can reach a conclusion" (160). Of course, progress, whether it is scientific, technological, or social, is simply a journey, not a destination. Utopia is an aim, not a target, whether fictional or otherwise. Max Gaffer says that: "The enemy of uncertainty might think the answer lies in grammar" (248), adding that, in relation to daily life and common misperceptions of history: "Progress is formidable on short acquaintance - after a time its existence can't be proven" (248). This pricks the bubble of orthodox religion, too. Violaine contributes: "Yield to doubt and glimpse a world of possibilities" (228).

Clearly, Accomplice does not fare well if its disordered society is measured up against any rough tick-box listing of utopian ideals:

- World peace and government based upon secular democracy

- Free education and universal healthcare for all "from cradle to grave"

- Humane population controls and euthanasia on demand

- Zero tolerance of capitalism/corporations to ennoble global civilization

- 100 percent "unemployment" so that nobody is forced to work for a living

Even the demonic spawn of hell disagree, on moral/ethical grounds, about a political philosophy, as Sweeney's prime agent provocateur Dietrich Hammerwire argues with the sympathetic-to-humanity Gettysburg:

"Autonomy is one tooth, useless." (182)

"You're wrong, it's owning your own jaws." (182)

The world's political systems are corrupt not because of the people that are currently in power, but because they are based on taxes and capitalism. Accomplice illustrates this fact by the seeming absence of money in its social order. The local economies of advanced biotech (such as the "seeds" that grow into a temporary courthouse, and the mayfly judge), and off-beat cultural exercises (like a Miasma festival and the Plunder parade), seems to be based upon unethical recycling, common thieving, and perhaps a kind of convoluted barter system with implied rewards that operates like karma. Is it utopian? No, but its elementary form of pragmatic anarchism is nevertheless quite appealing.

When poor Gregor receives a summons to court, his lawyer explains legal procedures in martial, medical, and philosophical or psychiatric terms:

"One of the big guns in the court's armory is its sedative effect. Bigger is its dismissal of objective reality and biggest, its ability to abduct people without moving a muscle - the abductees do all the work, tranced by assumed authority" (246).

Still, as Max Gaffer observes, "People will do almost anything to avoid acknowledging that they're powerless. That's a sturdy handle." (247) And so we lurch from social chaos to a moral crisis as, in class warfare, money and knowledge is power, and power corrupts. Dietrich proclaims, while asking the Mayor for a job, that apology gambits have "the element of surprise, and a fairly long rhetoric decay rate" (266). It's easy for him to say, but "There's the philosophy of politics, and there's the career of politics... Where the two meet, the process and machinery of politics is excreted."(266). The punch-line, of course, means that politicians like Rudloe are full of shit. Moreso when considering the worth of a mayoral blessing in Accomplice: "That statement was only local - in fact it did not persist beyond the room" (270). Such is the value and significance of a politician's promise.

DAMNATION TAKES

Concluding the Accomplice series, *Karloff's Circus* (287-379) is an account of what happens when a bizarre carnival of errors steams into town. It is not necessarily a pretty sight - with malevolent clowns, zombified trapeze acrobats, exploited and bewildered animal performers, a "tar baby" boxing match (the perfect job for Gregor, of course), and a local volunteer for the shot-from-a-cannon stunt. However, this all-consuming big-top jamboree of madness is par for the course in the absurdist realm of Accomplice, a town where everyone's in it together, but "Death is never at stake" (308).

It begins with the "suicide" of mechanic Mike Abblatia, leaving Accomplice - "the only town capable of being complicated by laziness" (289) - because his garage business is failing due to cars being stolen on a daily basis. It is as if the sharing if not caring community adheres to Pierre-Joseph Proudhon's anarchistic (18th century) political philosophy that "property is theft", at least as far as vehicle ownership and misuse is concerned.

The touring company of Karloff Velocet arrive via ghost train, bringing a freight of archly twisted fears to Accomplice which echoes the pandemonium carnival in Ray Bradbury's *Something Wicked This Way Comes* (1962). The circus delivers a dark reign of "accidents with accompaniment" (306) and upsets the townspeople with new challenges and unwanted reminiscence. Karloff is a galling opportunist with a yen for death and "a laugh that's hollow enough to shelter a fugitive" (308). Politically, he offers yet another shade of anarchy to Accomplice, and seems a fit antagonist for heroic Barny (who stole the circus's lion), and Karloff suggests forming an entertainment double–act with Rudloe (who attempts to steal the circus's thunder).

When Karloff visits the Mayor's offices, they discuss terms for Rudloe's participation/showmanship, but Rudloe is wary of forming a new alliance "in the full gape of public scrutiny" (320) and concerned that circus related antics may dilute the election campaign's message and undermine the image of himself that he would like to present. Karloff, to his merit, quotes from Violaine: "For propaganda to resist erosion, calm voices must be seen as more absurd than hysterical ones" (320). This calls to mind almost any example of political debating strategy between leftie and rightwing candidates found in living memory. Even the baker in the town's cake shop has something to say about society's deployment of agitprop in adverts: "Propaganda is buried in the greatest desirability," (327) he says to the easily perplexed Gregor.

During negotiations for the mayoral act in his circus, ringmaster Karloff observes that Rudloe's "stone bald misrule requires such occasional charm offensives" (330). But, like the best of enemies at the worst of

152

times, they are unable to reach a mutual agreement for a suitable act embracing "calamitous mayhem and insane megalomania" (331). Despite his willingness to co-operate, Rudloe fails in his aims to achieve a folksy popularity under the chapter heading of "Helterpolitik". Karloff has already established a pact with king demon Sweeney, and hints about their plans are found in the spell-casting credo that says: "Reform changes the shape of injustice" (334). Having test-fired his weapon of choice, Karloff, ever aspiring to be the very picture of talking villainy, explains his own goals, in a formal aggrandizement with a self–fulfilling prophecy:

I have a false crisis planned for the purpose of subsequent complacency. And my cover is perfect... dispensing aspersions like an ecclesiast. Horror is expected, and horror it shall be (334).

ALL OUR YESTERWAYS

A jobsworth guard named Murdster at the Tower of Nowt admits that his only pay is: "carefully contrived documents of a threatening nature, bills of lading, and a shout upside the face" (335), which sounds rather like a critique of modern slavery in "Workfare" programs. If the British government's Department for Work and Pensions (DWP) can tag-team up with French IT consultants Atos, to undermine and exploit an entire benefits system, that is already means–tested, in order to practically enslave disabled or unemployable victims of an economic slump, it permits schemes that only support the kind of anonymous bullying that would otherwise be condemned in any society of conscience.

Dumfounded by his direly troubling circumstances, trapeze artist zombie Fang quotes Violaine: "Consensus is reality with the crusts cut off" (336). Such a grimly dark philosophy is one that conjures hellish visions of savage Conservative rule where any last crumbs of ethical behavior towards an impoverished electorate are abandoned, and the lack of any coherent opposition allows it to happen. As we lurch through this 21st century dystopia (crudely defined, not as the worst of all possible worlds, but simply as a time when the cowed-into-silence majority believe that their situation in society cannot get better), seemingly always on the cusp of a game–changing Singularity, let us consider whether doomed Eddie Gallo's campaign slogan: "Bless the ultimate strangeness" (337) is a worthwhile position, or whether unemployed lawyer Max Gaffer is right to give up all hope of catching election fever again.

After the Moral Fibre ("it's just traditional. Its function is primarily to distract and waste time" (341)) is stolen - again, Rudloe updates the Conglomerate: "my show of being folksy is understood by everyone to be mere pretense." Even a skeptical farmer that Rudloe greets remains a portrait of "the stampede toward incredulity" (341). But this only masks a widespread apathy. Rudloe's grimace is actually an expression of superiority that assumes triumph: "They understand that there is a threat to them, behind our blithe shite. You know, I suspect I could tell them the whole truth? And nothing would happen" (341). However, the Conglomerate replies: "They already know it - and either pretend otherwise or that they approve. That's what participation is, and why you can't truly call them victims" (341). Demon defector Gettysburg also draws upon the succinct wisdom of Violaine: "A virtuous path in the world doesn't cease to function, it's just obscured" (342). Although the newly acclimatized to humanity Dietrich corrects that: "Yeah, but a path obscured ceases to function" (342). Can good ideas or ideals be lost if they fall into disuse? Is the newfound appeal of Russian–born writer–philosopher Ayn Rand for American vice presidential candidate Paul Ryan a curse or a blessing? How much Orwellian "Newspeak" can be tolerated before society turns combustible?

If the recessions that set in like rancid concrete after the financial crises of 2008 was, at least partly, caused by two wars based on lies and fought on credit, it is abundantly clear that: "Only a spectator may inherit the riches of war – participants merely pick over the lessons" (347). During the rather one–sided boxing match, between hapless non–entity Gregor and a thuggish monstrosity named Trubshaw, even gambling Rudloe is caught by surprise when demon Dietrich condemns mayoral power and government authority for supporting such a travesty of gross injustice: "The potent theatre of lies and ignorance – this is the value of Parliament" (350).

Before he succumbs to assimilation into the vampiric collective of the Conglomerate, primed for glutinous feeding upon the heinous blood levy, Rudloe is quietly informed of his citizen's duty:

> **help us pretend we're not the bad guys. That you are not taxed under threat. That all are created equal. That our office is earned. That there is no luck or privilege. That there is justice (372).**

It reminds us of that most infamous of mental images of the Orwellian boot, stamping down (all the way, from 1984, to the present), if not forever, then for the foreseeable future, most certainly.

SCARY CARTOONS

Aylett's sophisticated literary techniques combine such quasi–narrative events with a medley of nightmarish images in highly creative prose. The four *Accomplice* volumes offer fiction that defies categorization; fiction that is, nevertheless, endlessly amusing, and so infinitely quotable, in its dazzlingly inventive blend of horrific tragedy, philosophical rants, and comic farce. In dissecting the corpse of political rhetoric for toothy nuggets of comedy gold, Aylett displays writing skills that are honed and engagingly allusive, delivering impressively surprising and humorously twisted wordplay on frequencies attuned to keen ridicule and satirical notation.

Totaling fewer than 380 pages, less is definitely more in *The Complete Accomplice*. The densely complex views of the Accomplice books might appear marginally insane on first reading, with such decidedly odd stuff as grand pianos animated like giant spiders, and throwaway one-liners that only attain an uncanny relevance with later repetition. But Aylett's bunch of lovesick misfits, curiously eminent weirdoes, and incomparable monsters, provide us with a sturdy handle on such richly neo–gothic misadventures, even when absurdly morbid goings–on are merely sketched into the chronicle's wildly psychedelic backgrounds

Works Cited

Aylett, Steve. *The Complete Accomplice*. London: Scar Garden Media, 2010.

"Paxman versus Howard". *Newsnight*. BBC Online Services. *BBC News*. United Kingdom. 13 May 1997. Television.

Verlaine, Tom. "Mr. Bingo." *Tom Verlaine*. Elektra, 1979. Vinyl recording.

Slaughtermatic: **Assault on Authority**

John Oakes

Once upon a time, while directing a small independent publishing house, I received a manuscript that, starting with its epigraph, announced itself as something very different and very funny:

"I think I'm hit."
—Baby Face Nelson, hit seventeen times by a .45 caliber Tommy gun

This was my introduction to *Slaughtermatic*'s Beerlight, a world where "to kill a man was less a statement than a mannerism" (xi). Appearing as it did in the post-punk era of 1995, when New York was suddenly less about rock 'n' roll, riots, and drugs than real estate, when all things alternative withered under the deceptively bland, vampiric regime of the Clinton Administration. The novel was a refreshing clarion call to the culturally defiant: violent, and violently funny; cynical, suffused with drugs and guns, and best of all, strictly speaking the plot didn't make sense. It was itself a cultural weapon: it seemed to me as dangerous in real-life as *The Impossible Plot of Biff Barbanel*, the book which "nobody could read and live" (47), the poisonous treasure hidden in a bank safe that provides the impetus for the sea of blood spilled in *Slaughtermatic*. In its wake, so much that was seen then as daring or edgy - the work of the Bret Easton Ellises, the T.C. Boyles and David Foster Wallaces - appeared tame, predictable and academic. I loved *Slaughtermatic*, and was certain it would shortly be found at the bedside table of every American.

The Crime Lord behind this mayhem was a young English writer hailing from the obscure London suburb of Bromley, unheralded by the intelligentsia, published by a UK house even smaller than the one that I ran. Steve Aylett resided then, as he still does, behind tinted glasses, and seemed to be permanently welded to a combination of a long black coat and a horizontally-striped shirt. A Beckett of psychedelia: a laconic jeweler of hitherto-unseen and unimagined phrases.

In *Slaughtermatic*, Aylett takes the pulp novel, a noir icon so time-worn that even the parodies have parodies, and amazingly, spectacularly, creates an original, readable, literary sci-fi amalgam. Genuine precedents? Shades of James M. Cain, Philip K. Dick, and William S. Burroughs do emerge in some passages, but throughout his book Aylett scatters, jewel-like, sentences and concepts never before encountered:

"Specter thought fondly of the days when he'd tear off the eyebrow of a witness and blow it towards the jury like the seed-head of a dandelion" (82).

"Surrender now and I'll forget I ever said this" (147).

"Love sure burned a layer off your expectations. 'He who fights and runs away,' he thought, ramming through a roadblock, 'than never to have loved at all'" (152).

Aylett toys with cliché and idiom, and he toys with toying: and at the same time, with this total embrace of artifice, he touches on the real. Aylett imbibes storytelling and spits out something genuine.

We rely on evoking images of the familiar for quick transmittal. That's true for the written vocabulary as well as the visual: we "read" words, pixels on a page, recognizing shapes of letters that form the words that form the phrases, the familiar combination that leads to an impression of understanding, and skim over details to what we think is actual meaning. Aylett understands and subverts our forgetfulness. In the course of doing so, he has opened up a new dimension of literature.

The heist launches the book. No explanation needed here. Shades of vintage Americana are immediately discernible: soulful, doomed hero Dante Cubit wields a Winchester shotgun (a nod to classic Westerns) but really wants to discuss economics or poetry; his equally morose sidekick the Entropy Kid, "almost amphibious with despair" pops pills and carries a "Kafkacell cannon gun" presided over by the Kid's light trigger-finger (3). Their hostage the "perky" bank teller is another stock character, a gum-chewing moll from an Edward G. Robinson flick who fixates on the Kid. We now have been introduced to our alternative Hole-in-the-Wall gang, shortly augmented by one Download Jones, the techno mastermind who has supplied the plans of the bank building and vault, and Rosa Control – the black leather-clad love of Dante's life, Cat Woman-like and irresistible, in every sense of that word.

Dante heads to the vault wherein lie the safe deposit boxes, one of which holds the aforementioned *Impossible Plot* by the mythic Eddie Gamete. A straightforward stickup? Hardly. The bank vault's "time lock" has been subverted by Jones, so that instead of throwing a thief twenty minutes into the future when the police have arrived, as it is supposed to, it throws Dante twenty minutes into the past – when he, now Dante Two, can appear on the bank floor to surprise the guards just before the stick-up occurs and Dante One arrives along with the Kid. It's a bit complicated: but does Aylett shirk from such challenges? No, he makes it worse: to avoid confusion and the possible immolation of all Beerlight (it's a physics thing) should Dante remain a multiplication of himself, Dante One shoots Dante Two in the stomach . . . and turns away, thinking he's killed his doppelgänger (or is Dante One the doppelgänger?). As the foregoing implies: he hasn't. More on that later.

Heading to the roof to make their getaway, the robbers find they've memorized the wrong building plans, and Dante One, undoubtedly the sort prone to depression under the sunniest of skies, slumps to the ground, suspecting his life is a fiction, that he is caught in a virtual feedback loop – that in "reality," or "meat-time" his mind is being held in electronic purgatory, his body imprisoned by the authorities for various sins in a holding tank known as the "Mall." Is the stick-up part of an endless, and therefore pointless, litany of slaughter? Has he, and by implication the reader, been fed a souped-up Shaggy Dog Story, another American trope incorporated by Aylett?

Re-reading *Slaughtermatic*, I am put in mind of the Irish critic and philosopher Denis Donoghue, who in *Ferocious Alphabets* quotes Plato quoting Socrates quoting an ancient legend concerning a mighty Egyptian king who is approached by a god, Thoth, known to us today primarily for sporting the head of a dog-faced baboon or, at times, an ibis. Ibis-headed or baboon-headed Thoth lays before the king a series of gifts, one more magnificent than the next. Finally, he presents the king his greatest gift: an invention he says is the key to furthering humanity's wisdom, its memory and therefore its understanding of the universe. The gift, of course, is writing. The king demurs: whether out of error or malice, Thoth has ascribed to letters "a power that is the opposite of what they really possess" (Donoghue 94). Writing contributes to confusion, to the gloss of understanding that leads to spiritual and physical mayhem; it is meaning's doppelgänger diverting us from the true path. Thoth, now perhaps recognizable as a trickster (his Greek counterpart Hermes, god of thieves, poets, and commerce, has long been identified as such) does not respond.

Next on the scene: the brotherhood, Beerlight's gang of officialdom otherwise known as "police," roars up to the bank. Here Aylett introduces us to one of his most intriguing creations: Chief Harry Blince, brutal, powerful and fat, an unredeemable, joyously violent creature recalling Captain Hank Quinlan (Orson Welles' role in *Touch of Evil*). Abetted in his cruelties by his slightly less fearsome amanuensis Benny the Trooper, the jester to his mad king (and if the king is mad, the jester, at once partner and antidote to the regal, is at least somewhat sane), Blince, a doughnut devotee and firm believer in the virtues of pre-emptive strikes, promptly sets about mowing down the bank employees.

Rosa Control, concerned for her Dante's well-being, pays Download Jones a visit in his lair: it turns out that Benny and Blince are the ones caught in the virtual feedback loop; they've been captured by Jones and fed endless visions of violence and chaos. At this point, things get more than a little hazy.

The police burst in: they free their comrades-in-arms and nab Jones. Rosa makes a getaway. Blince and co. hurry off to the "real" bank job. Back at the brotherhood's den, Jones is interrogated but "volunteers nothing but fluids." Of course, he retains several secrets: an explosive one buried in his body is relevant to this particular moment in the book:

> **Download was pounded to the floor. He moved his arm as though he'd the temerity to protect himself. In what form would his atonement come to fruition? They refused to tell him, feigning bafflement. A fist smashed into his jaw and, with a sound louder than a bomb, the building vaporized so fast a dozen bigots were left falsifying evidence in mid-air. (32)**

Parse the above; it contains several of the elements that make *Slaughtermatic* an outstanding work. There is direct physical action: our man is dropped to the floor. We know something of him; he's the one person identified by name in the interrogation - the others are "they," faceless figures of authority - we can't help but sympathize with him, the hunted, the victim, the one human. There is tenderness, a delicate evocation of pain without crudely specifying its source - Download Jones may be a criminal but he is no assassin, he's a classic geek, and it makes sense he'd shield himself from violence. By the standards of Beerlight he should expect, perhaps even welcome suffering in the face of the brotherhood's wrath; thus defending himself is courageous and unexpected. How can he ever pay for what he has done? But the police mock him, and continue the torture. Download's self-destruct mechanism is set off. In martyrdom, the geek emerges triumphant. Throughout the novel, this combination of poetically expressed humanity and over-the-top violence lifts the prose out of the realm of gonzo/bizarro writing and into the sublime.

Outside the besieged bank, Blince encounters Officer Tredwell Garnishee, who exhibits slight and, to the chief, disturbing strains of lawfulness and sincerity. But his real sin, in Blince's eyes, is in serving him inferior doughnuts: "You're a waste of hair, Tredwell. You wouldn't make an impression on a goddamn pillow" (35). Blince fires him and proceeds to kill everything in and out of sight, making up for the fact that his previous slaughter of innocent bystanders took place only in virtual reality. Meanwhile, leaving Dante One behind—despite their entreaties, he listlessly refuses to join them—the Kid and Cory the Teller make their way to the roof of the bank building, where they flee by clinging to inflatable dictators that have been warehoused on a floor above the bank. Benny looks upward to witness their escape: "Eight Hitlers, three Napoleons and a Mao emerged and began floating upward like a soap bubble cluster. Suspended beneath them was the Entropy Kid and a cackling woman" (40).

It transpires that Dante Two has survived his gut shot: he wanders Beerlight forlornly, bleeding and searching for Rosa. And poor cashiered Tredwell, never really off the case, has an unfortunate encounter with a bloodthirsty lawyer (perhaps Aylett's only flirtation with cliché, but a well-placed one) and is shot. Propelled by duty alone, he staggers to the offices of the rent-a-hitman entrepreneur Hustler Meese. His last, selfless act is to engage the assassin Brute Parker to kill Dante: Tredwell believes that if the two Dantes meet in real-time the result will be a massive explosion laying waste to all of Beerlight.

But Dante Two survives even Parker's expert and enthusiastic attempts at annihilation, and towards the end of the book the two Dantes do get together for a lively, non-violent verbal tussle (throughout which they are careful not to touch one another). They have an exchange that provides a clue that of the two Dantes, the "real" one, the one which retains the grim, vinegary essence of the original, is Dante Two—despite the fact he's a replication. By copying himself, Dante One has become a sunnier, lamer iteration, the dregs: the proof is that he prefers a trashy 1992 remake (starring Drew Barrymore) of the 1950 film *Gun Crazy* (directed by Joseph H. Lewis) which Dante Two disdains, preferring the decidedly noir original.

Much is blown up in *Slaughtermatic*, but it would be a mistake to think this anarchy for anarchy's sake: it is constructive destruction. In the wake of Aylett's verbal demolition, an alien, delicate structure emerges. The preposterous names, the outrageous and cartoon-like antics of Beerlight's denizens lie like a mask over Aylett's refinement and precision. This is a book about a book, a book about lovers of books and love—Dante and Rosa are the star-crossed couple essential to any gunslingers' tale—an ode to all that is noir.

Works Cited

Aylett, Steve. *Slaughtermatic*. New York: Four Walls
    Eight Windows, 1997.

Donoghue, Denis. *Ferocious Alphabets*. New York:
    Columbia University Press, 1984

Aylett Entry

Rhys Hughes

I dithered a lot over writing this short text. I could say I was deliberately late in finishing and submitting it in order to justify calling it 'Aylett Entry,' but titles don't really need that sort of justification, and I often give untrue titles to pieces of work, so the excuse would fool nobody. And even if his surname was *Anurly* it would still be late. Right from the start, when first asked to do something on Steve Aylett, I couldn't imagine how to proceed, and so I initially declined the task. "What we cannot speak of we should pass over in silence."

But passing over in silence is unsatisfactory.

It occurred to me that maybe I could write a piece about *how* and *why* I felt unable to write about Steve Aylett. He has that strange effect on me. Most writers don't.

I think the first time I heard the words 'Steve Aylett' was from the mouth of Michael Moorcock. I can't be certain about this but it wouldn't surprise me because Moorcock's recommendations have introduced me to more wonderful writers over the years than anyone else's.

Aylett was surely one of those. I hearkened.

But it took a while before I managed to obtain an Aylett book, and when I did it was another few months before I actually sat down and read it. Only a few months. That's a very short time between obtaining and digesting. Normally the obtaining precedes the digesting by years.

This is due to the immense length of my "To Read" list. I own more books that I will ever read in my lifetime. They are stacked on shelves and stuffed into boxes in cupboards and hidden under the bed and crammed into the corners. I possess books that have been waiting twenty years or more to be read. Therefore, it's unusual for a new author to jump the queue and get one of his books near the top of the list.

But Aylett managed it somehow. The book was *Lint*. For me it is the perfect novel of its kind.

The spoof biography has a long and illustrious history. The invented SF writer with a ludicrous career has been done before, many times, and for most people Kilgore Trout, the dour creation of Kurt Vonnegut that was appropriated by Philip José Farmer, is the obvious example.

Kilgore Trout is an amusing and necessary invention.

But Jeff Lint, hero of *Lint*, is the eidolon of the type. Aylett takes further the basic conceit, makes it funnier, crasser, darker, wider, stranger, and trumps Vonnegut in every essential way. Lint replaces Trout as the true Quixote of the pulp universe, he is the best and soundest frame for the satire that clothes him, a satire that is simultaneously cutting and endearing.

When I started reading the book, not too long after it was published, there seemed to be lots and lots of emerging writers in the speculative fiction world all named Jeff. There was a plethora of Jeffs. Pure coincidence, naturally, but the addition of this other Jeff, this fictional absurd lunatic scribbler Jeff, into the Jeff-mêlée felt absolutely right and proper.

Many of those real Jeffs were bold pioneers who pushed fiction into new and exciting realms, but this fictional *sous-Jeff* was also a bold pioneer, a man who turned up in person to submit manuscripts to publishers while resentfully dressed as a majorette because he had misheard "Pop it through the mail, you know our address" as "Poppet, for a male you know how to dress" and thought that presentation was crucial in the business (203).

Lint is a vehicle for ideas, for conceits and concepts scattered about with gusto and immense generosity. The writing world, especially the genre writing world, is ripe, overripe indeed, for comical lambasting and has been lambasted many times over the decades, but never with quite such verve, such style, such informed and yet sympathetic savagery. The (deliberate) irony is that many of the notional projects of Jeff Lint are genuinely enthralling. So Aylett is able to scatter ideas like seeds, in the manner of Stanislaw Lem, without having to tend them and watch them grow into something else.

This is a very efficient but extremely difficult way of writing.

As Brian Aldiss has said, "Ideas are hard work."

The existence of *Lint* means that I will never have to write a satire along these lines. This is a relief, for I wouldn't be able to do it a tenth so well. It is a noble act when an author saves one from work beyond one's ability. Aylett has done this task superbly and is a true benefactor.

Works Cited

Aylett, Steve. *Lint*. New York: Thunder's Mouth Press, 2005.

Aylett's Inferno

Bill Ectric

"Of making many books there is no end,
and much study wearies the body."
- Ecclesiastes 12:12

Warning: Spoiler Alerts Galore

Ecclesiastes is unique among the books of the Bible. It boasts no giants, no flaming chariots, no Satan, and people all go to one place when they die – into the earth. Just the fact that this book is included in the Bible is a miracle in itself. Ecclesiastes is a mirror image to the rest of the canon because its viewpoint is mortal and earthly as opposed to divine and celestial, and that is why I thought of it while reading Steve Aylett's short novel *Shamanspace*, with its symbolism of the "mirror book," introduced early in the story and reappearing at regular intervals.

In *Shamanspace*, two rival factions, the Prevail and the Internecine, want to assassinate God. They are angry and indignant about all the suffering. The Prevail believe that if God dies, the universe will continue to exist, separate from the creator. The Internecine believe that upon God's death, the universe and everyone in it will be no more, and they consider that outcome "a small price to pay" (Aylett 119). Both factions have agents/assassins called "edgemen" who are capable of leaving their bodies and merging into matter, travelling as atom swarms along the planes of surfaces like

173

buildings, roads, and even air. Entering higher dimensions through hidden "angles" in the fabric of the universe, they move through cities unseen, like stealthy noir detectives. Edgemen can also enter other people's bodies and disguise themselves in "shell bodies" to go undercover in the normal world. People born with the DNA for edgework are detected, selected, and recruited by either the Prevail or Internecine for training.

The origin of the edgemen is explained in an Appendix at the end of *Shamanspace*. Aylett mixes actual history with his own fabricated events and characters, tracing an authentic-sounding timeline of religion, alchemy, astronomy, physics, secret societies, and intrigue. In a way, it reminds me of Eco's *Foucault's Pendulum* or Pynchon's *The Crying of Lot 49,* but, in classic Aylett style, condensed into a few pages and punctuated by sardonic humor. The Appendix contains just enough truth to seem logical, to give one the impression of discovering a secret history. "Slavers cross-fertilized Yezidism with toxic wicca during the Roman conquests, resulting in angry faces all around" (115), "…see Basil Valentine's ironically codified text *The Triumphal Chariot*, in which cypher generates the request 'Just kill me' more often than the number of words in the manuscript" (117).

Some readers will be appalled by the idea of "killing God" and may prefer to see *Shamanspace* as metaphor for the suicidal urge (more on that later) or a commentary on the arrogance of deluded mortals. As always happens when I read Aylett, several thoughts went through my mind. I thought of Nietzsche's "God is dead" spiel, and how one of my high school teachers tried to play it down by saying that Nietzsche was only commenting on the growing trend toward atheism. In that regard, she was correct; Nietzsche did not believe

God was dead because he did not believe in God. His message was that when people realize they no longer have God as a standard, they either become stronger and take responsibility for themselves, or become nihilistic and open to despair. Of course, you don't have to lose your faith to be nihilistic. The author of Ecclesiastes moans about "all the days of his meaningless life which he spends as a shadow" (Ecclesiastes 14), but he does seem to rally in the last chapter and ends on an encouraging note. *Shamanspace* also reminded me of Greek mythology; specifically the story of how giants tried to overthrow Zeus, throwing rocks and flaming trees at him. Zeus turned to Heracles to help him defeat the giants. But let us return to the immediate plot.

The book's Preface introduces two edgemen as they navigate South London, flowing through angular dimensions of "otherspace" on a quest. One of them is Sig, a trainee, young and inexperienced. The other is Melody, a French girl and a well-tuned veteran. Their goal is for Sig to meet Alix, a "living legend" among their kind, for Sig to glean whatever information or advice he can from the damaged hero. Alix had been a brilliant edgeman. "They said Alix could enter the face of a guitar without making a sound" (Aylett 14), but now he was burned out. "(Alix's) eyes were turns of liquid gold, glistening and unseeing" (16). Eyes like liquid metal is a recurring characteristic of edgemen who have gone off the deep end.

Aylett's vibrant prose makes the action super-vivid. Sometime I followed the literal plot of the story, but there are impressionistic passages I cannot quite put into words. Some of the impressions I will share in this essay may or may not reflect Aylett's intended meaning.

Legendary Alix tells young Sig his story, beginning in Chapter One. He recounts how he once entered a bar, disguised in a shell body, "self-brainwashed so that a mind-reading enemy would still be fooled" (Questions). In the bar, he meets a girl, also a disguised assassin, and a doomed relationship begins. He is Internecine; she is Prevail. Spy and detective stories are brimming with men and women from enemy camps getting together for a tangled mix of attraction and espionage. "We went up in a cage elevator somewhere. Her hair hides the phone. After that I lost track of time for a while" (Aylett 22). He wakes up in someone's apartment. Alix is so deep undercover he has forgotten who he is. He's been "washing one drug down with another" (21), but a vague memory stirs an instinctive impulse. There is a smudged stamp on his wrist – the kind they stamp on you when you enter a bar – and Aix slits his wrist at that spot.

It is here that we examine the parallel meanings in Aylett's work. I've written before about Aylett's work having at least three meanings at once. On one level, Alix could be a weary man, tired of living in the fast lane, wanting to end it all. On another level, maybe he is using the knife blade to "wake himself up" or shock himself back to the reality of who he is. Think of the lyrics by Trent Reznor, "I hurt myself today, to see if I still feel" (Nine Inch Nails). Perhaps he needed to cut an exit wound to leave the shell body behind. All these things can be true at the same time. It's like the Interzone concept of William S. Burroughs, as distilled by David Cronenberg in the film *Naked Lunch*; Bill Lee may be an Inspector on a mission in the Interzone to track down members of the Nova Mob, or he might be a drug addict moving through the streets and alleys of

Tangier, Morocco to track down smack. Or both, simultaneously.

Alix gets his bearings and finds the girl asleep in a back room, suspended in a "biomechanical bag, like a cocoon or a closed hammock, which she uses to maintain herself" (Questions). She is an undercover assassin (so is he). He slices open the cocoon and accesses her brain for secrets, any intelligence she may have gathered that would facilitate the mission of locating and assassinating God. In the process, he picks up memories of her childhood, of getting ostracized for being different, able to see things that were invisible to ordinary people: "structures in events…armatures of human need and fantasy anglepoising between the people, linking them in a jagged scaffold" (Aylett 24), her dreams crushed, scooped up by the Prevail as a trainee, and something else: Alix recognized her as a human being. "Something of herself was left, a miniscule mischief which rifled a secret and took it away. Sacred telemetry" (25). The girl dies as her secret thoughts rush into Alix's brain. It is not clear if this was intentional on his part, and Alix is racked with sobs. He had seen her beauty, identified with her pain, his guilt and sense of loss. It's interesting that in one sentence, there seems to be a moment of shared thought. We look at the words, "Something of herself was left, a miniscule mischief which rifled a secret (25)," so her mischief included rifling secrets, just as he is rifling secrets from her, and for a brief moment, the middle of that sentence applies to both her and him simultaneously. This is how he obtains the coordinates to the heart of God.

Back at Internecine headquarters, known as "the Keep," Alix needs some recovery time. Exercising one's power as an edgeman takes a toll on a person. Physical and emotional. "I was ghostburnt, in mourning and voiding lumps of the cover personality" (29). After a few days, he is sitting in the office of his boss, Lockhart, who is like a father to Alix, for a kind of debriefing. Lockhart tells Alix that Melody is in France, spying on the Prevail headquarters there. They wonder, if the Prevail know the location of God's heart, why haven't they made the "hit." Is it pity? Procrastination? Are they afraid of failure or afraid of what will happen if they succeed? Lockhart wants Alix to visit Quinas, a veteran "has-been" edgeman who is kept in a cell under guard because he is insane. Alix does not relish this suggestion. "I've met shamanic burnouts. Some shivering leftover with weird eyes? I haven't got the patience to hear about some gold-rimmed yesterday" (33). But Alix acquiesces and goes to see Quinas:

> **I went through the ivied gate to the locked quarters, a guard allowing entry. Quinas was meant to be batshit crazy and acquitted himself well. He sat at the center of his cell like an albino frog, working on some obscure cabbalistic grid, probably a malice puzzle. Proceeding around him was a polychrome exchange, the walls trancing with sickly refractions. His head was sprouted with white death-hairs, and when he turned my way I saw his eyes were liquid mercury, the surfaces flowing like oily water (39).**

Alix meeting Quinas can be seen as Alix looking at a mirror image of what he might someday be, just like Sig meeting Alix in the preface of the book.

Quinas suggests that if God is everything, and we are a part of God, then we are God's suicidal impulse. He tells Alix, "God made us conscious for a reason. It knew that when its cells became self-aware, they'd experience a pitch of pain that'd send them for revenge. We're nano-assassins" (45).

Quinas gives Alix a book as a going-away gift. It is a book of mirrors called "Acqueville's *Flightless Land Without Clouds*" (46). As Alix is leaving with the book, he stops just outside the door and glances back to see Quinas flickering and fading from sight. Quinas then emerges from the mirror book as a red electric outline and escapes into the city.

Alix track Quinas to Paris, where the Prevail headquarters is located. "This suggested (Quinas) had some business with the Prevail," says Alix. "I should have known when he referred to the world as God's 'moulted material' – Prevail philosophy" (51). Alix joins Melody in a safe house in the Rue Fromentin. With his edgeman-heightened awareness of connections between essence and matter, he is unnerved by the "left-handed landscapes and cathedrals brittle as candy" (51). The cathedral description is apt - if you look at the Notre Dame Cathedral in Reims, the Russian Orthodox Cathedral in Nice, or the Metz Cathedral in Lorraine, they do have a cake-decoration-confectionary-sugar delicacy. The "left-handed landscape" comment is a little less clear, an example of Aylett's impressionist style. To me, it brings to mind the Left Bank of Paris and the traditional "otherness" often attributed to France. The Right Bank of the Seine River is where one finds big businesses and professional buildings, an environment closer to the cityscape of Alix's exploits in London. The Left Bank is traditionally for bohemian artists and writers (to overgeneralize).

Alix asks Melody for directions to the Prevail motherhouse (headquarters) and:

She pointed in the 9th direction. I took a very deliberate half-turning step which tilted an edge in the air, showing me a dense cross-section of several etheric miles. I raised an arm toward it, the funhouse-mirror limb stretching to infinity, and let it draw the rest of me into subspace like an elastic band (52).

At the Prevail motherhouse, an invisible Alix sees Casolaro, head of the Prevail, talking to Quinas, the turncoat, consorting with the enemy. As they talk, a young edgeman, Moon, senses Alix's presence. Alix retreats as Moon crosses over into the etheric zone in pursuit. A splendid chase ensues.

Passing the mouth of an alley, I folded down to a single element and streamed sideways into the architecture…Moon sifted in also and we were fleshtones flushing through the walls on either side of the alley – branching up into roofs and undoing bundles of air before dipping into masonry again (57).

I won't describe the entire chase, but it ends when:

(Alix) slammed to a stop inside a car, slipped upward through the roof and apported, jumping down to the tarmac. Moon materialized too fast, merging with a Volvo – the windows were instantly painted red from the inside and shattered as metal warped out (58).

After resting up in Melody's hotel room, Alix decides to take his mirror book to a nearby antique bookshop. Alix is saying goodbye to his world before carrying out the hit, and his love of books is evident. I never tire of Aylett's descriptions of books, bric-a-bac, and curiosities.

> **Here and there were books produced by cabinet-makers, passwords under the blurbs... Spreading the mirror pages to those of the old books, reflections showed the snail trail left by the author's bile, invisible behind the print. 'Our secret broken law,' a law so irretrievably broken it had to be retroactively denied. *Medicine is the Slightest Species of Magic*, the true title of a treatise on the Napoleonic wars...tasting hidden chapter names behind the visible...(62-63)**

Alix reflects on his life, possibly for the last time:

> **Picking up history like coloured flavors... railway furnaces, chestnut anciency, pistol cloaks, hooded horses in a dark tunnel, a symphony of something through long corridors of wide avenues... a seat by the shore... chairflap beaches of afternoons... children at a distance change, yellowing, momentariness (63-64).**

He returns to the hotel, where he and Melody inject tears into their arms to experience hallucinogenic ecstasy. Blissful intimacy. When Melody is asleep, Alix prepares to enter the heart of God for the kill, aided by directions he pilfered from the girl in the cocoon back in the first chapter. But before he can take off, someone strikes him from behind, knocking him unconscious, and he is kidnapped by the Prevail.

He wakes up on a Prevail sub called the Bluetooth, confined in a sarcophagus-like box that blocks his power to flow through matter. The sub brings him back to England. I won't recount his escape, but suffice it to say, he ends up back at the Internecine headquarters – the Keep. He finds Lockhart, his boss, who seems strangely uncomfortable. Alix talks about the irony that both factions, Prevail and Internecine, want to assassinate the same target, yet they continually delay one another. He has a theory as to why this stalemate exists. "(The Prevail) think we're out to stage-manage the death of the universe," he tells Lockhart, "whether it ensues naturally from God's death or not" (77). He is correct about the Prevail's concerns, but his theory hasn't gone far enough. Apparently the Prevail have persuaded the Internecine to see it their way. Alix is shocked to see Casolaro, the Prevail leader, enter the room, soon followed by Quinas, and someone named Dreva, "a young Prevail techy and strongarm" (82). It seems that Lockhart, the Internecine leader, has joined forces with Casolaro and Quinas behind Alix's back. Quinas no longer seems like a burnout, "looking smart and healthy in a white leather coat, his death-hair slicked back to the skull" (82, 83). Weakened from his recent exertion, Alix is unable to prevent them from fastening him to:

> **an upright aura-rack at the far end of the chamber. The motherhouse basement was an etheric runway. The old ascension containment cross had been dragged out of**

> **storage and stood on the cocoon platform between amplifier housings. The cross was an ancient but effective trip preventer which worked in part by keeping the subject spread and unable to focus inward – like trying to sing low with your head high. An electrostatic discharge closed the etheric airlocks and threw me back against the main spar. It was Saturday morning (82).**

Obvious imagery of Jesus on the cross here. It's possible that the mention of Saturday morning is, if not merely one of Aylett's non sequiturs, a way of saying Alix was poised halfway between Good Friday, when Jesus was crucified, and Easter Sunday, when he was resurrected.

"You think it's coincidental," asks Quinas, "that at precisely the time that the greatest number of people feel indignant at God's works, the fewest ever people believe in it?" (86)

Alix realizes that his captors aren't so much worried about the world ending as they are simply "bone scared" (86) of making God angry.

"We're reduced to stupid intrigues," chides Alix, "hitting each other around the head in hotel rooms – the First Mystic Renegades would be ashamed" (87).

Melody enters the room, apparently part of the betrayal.

Casolaro approaches Alix with a hypodermic containing a fatal dose of poison.

Melody hands an old book to Quinas.

Quinas opens the book with casual curiosity.

> **Melody had put the mirror book into an old cover. A scream tore in half as Quinas was**

> **drawn eyes-first into the object, a cloud of
> blood sizzling across the floor and ceiling,
> drenching the onlookers. Casolaro looked
> back as Melody whacked down the generator
> switch, breaking the current to the rack (96).**

It is interesting that the etheric containment device is referred to as both a rack and a cross. Ironic that Medieval church states employed the rack to compel heretics to confess.

With the containment device disengaged, Alix quickly launches his etheric essence free from his body and into higher dimensions, hurtling into God's domain to carry out the hit.

Alix finally approaches the heart of God, within striking distance.

He is horrified:

> **But when the thing grew near, it precipitated
> from all directions in a vastness of intricate,
> nonrepeating evil. A slow spectacle of dark
> vanes and complex underside…(103)**

Several interpretations went through my mind as this passage unfolded, much quicker than it will take to write about them.

The first interpretation is simply that Alix is looking at God, and if that is the case, then the Almighty is god-awful:

> **a titanic black insect floundered on its back
> at the center of an infinite nerve net, fiddling
> a millions legs amid the ferocious stench of
> vomit and scorching wires (103).**

In 1976, psychologist Julian Jaynes proposed the theory of the *bicameral mind*. He believed that up until a few thousand years ago, when one side of our brain 'spoke' to the other side, early humans did not recognize the thoughts as coming from their own mind. After reading Jaynes' book, Rabbi James Cohn wrote *The Minds of the Bible*, suggesting that Old Testament accounts of people "hearing the voice of God" are explained by the bicameral mind theory, and that is why we rarely hear of this phenomenon today (except in the case of schizophrenics). In this light, one could infer that the mirror imagery in *Shamanspace* is symbolic of Alix looking deep into his own monstrous psyche.

> **Its mouth rimmed with lashes like an eye, biting in space at an end, it was eternally frantic in its convulsions, evils tangling and stretching about its mindless ratcheting (103).**

Or, maybe both things are true, that God is our mind but is also a god who exists separate from each individual, in a "wave or particle" construct. Carl Jung coined the term "collective unconscious" as a way of saying all people share universal symbols, or archetypes, in the DNA of our subconscious minds. But it goes further than that. Some researchers have applied Erwin Schrödinger's unified field theory to the functions of the brain, based on the generally accepted fact that our thoughts generate from a physical process of chemical and electrical synapses. In this way, our minds are truly connected, not just by sharing the same unconscious archetypes, but joined in a quantum grid along with space, time, and mass. This may be what we call God, living inside and outside our brains at the same time.

> **Shackled by its own influence. Seeping cold
> corrosion in a night of oceanic tragedy. No
> cure ever, a constantly breaking heart.**
> **And before this thing I felt the blossoming
> of total exposure. All resolves atomized by
> horror. One particle of poison in a sea of
> poison. No guts in a zero. No hero.**
> **On the cross, my eyes turned to gold (103).**

A mirror image of Christ, perhaps? Christians believe God came to Earth and allowed us to kill him. Alix went chasing God. Both ended on a cross. Both were still alive at the end of the book.

I emailed Steve Aylett, asking, "When Alix finally sees God, is he simply too appalled to kill it? Or too anguished or broken-hearted, with the brokenness feeding back into him?"

Steve's reply was, "Yes, Alix is overwhelmed by the horror of that vision, and the fact that the god insect seems to be tangled and caught in its own horror. Alix experiences a universe-sized depressive breakdown" (RE: Questions).

And his eyes turned to gold, like the others.

Alix finishes his story in tears and Sig is awestruck, saying, "But you are sort of a hero. You found the heart despite everything, everyone."

Alix tells Sig:

> **You don't get it…the whole thing was stage-
> managed. The whole deal had been to send
> me off with passion. My friends. To save me
> from being a mere dry aeronaut, easily
> turned. Quinas knew he'd get it in the neck -
> but he welcomed it as a burnout. He had**

more mischief in him at the end than a lot of us start out with (107-108).

But Sig doesn't quite believe it. He is a young gun with stars in his eyes, chomping at the bit for front-line action, to take on God and finish the job.

Melody stands in the doorway and Alix, now blind, senses her presence. He tells her, "I know it's you brings the flowers" (109). This is a touching scene and makes me lean toward the theory that *Shamanspace* is a metaphor for a suicide attempt. Waking up in a hospital room.

But, no. I'm with Sig. I want to believe in super-powered edgemen flowing through matter and into other dimensions.

Peter Wild, in his review of *Shamanspace* on *Bookmunch*, compares the end of the book to "coming down from a trip" (Wild), and I agree. The book enthralled me, heightened my senses, and although nothing had changed, I felt different when it was over. I think of the old Zen axiom, "Before enlightenment, I chopped wood and carried water. After enlightenment, I chopped wood and carried water."

Aylett told me, "It's understandable that *Shamanspace* is hard to understand at times, Bill - it's my most obscure and tortuous book, all meaning and no jokes. It's sort of the opposite of *The Inflatable Volunteer*, which was all jokes and no meaning. It's informed by total agony and despair" (RE: Questions).

"God is a concept by which we measure our pain."
– John Lennon

Works Cited

Aylett, Steve. *Shamanspace*. UK: Codex Books, 2001.

Ecclesiastes, or, the Preacher. The Pocket Canon Series. New York: Grove Press/Atlantic, 1999. Print.

Lennon, John. "God." *John Lennon/Plastic Ono Band.* Apple, 1970.Vinyl record.

Nietzsche, Friedrich. *Thus Spoke Zarathustra: A Book for All and None.* Trans R. J. Hollingdale. UK: Penguin Classics, 1961. Print.

Nine Inch Nails. "Hurt." *The Downward Spiral.* Nothing/Interscope Records, 1994. CD.

"RE: Questions about *Shamanspace*." Message to Bill Ectric. 10 June 2015. Email.

Wild, Peter. "Books You Should've Read By Now." *Bookmunch.* 19 June 2016. 20 June 2016.

Introduction to *Fain the Sorcerer*

Alan Moore

If we loved Steve Aylett, really loved him in the way that
he deserves, a selfless love that genuinely wanted
nothing save his happiness and comfort, we'd
lobotomize him. Nothing complicated or too costly, just
a well-judged swipe with shovel blade or flat iron when
he isn't looking ought to do the trick. This would afford
him satisfaction in more ways than one. Firstly, it would
confirm his previous opinion of us personally and of
humanity in general, and secondly it might impair him
mentally, thus furthering his career. If he could just stop
the Tourette's flood of original ideas, dilute the language
so the reader only had to pause and shake their head in
admiration every paragraph or so rather than every
other line, this man could be a sales phenomenon, could
be a franchise; it's all just a shovel-blow away. There
would be glowing twelve-year-olds lined up in
Waterstones at midnight for the latest Beerlight or
Accomplice saga, there'd be blockbusters, Jeremy
Paxman flirting openly with Aylett during *Newsnight*,
Lint confectionery, Hell toys. Best of all, with his critical
faculties all having gone the same way as his frontal
lobe, he'll have no idea that he's writing tepid drivel and
can just enjoy himself, can ride round Tunbridge Wells
in a gold dodgem car, eating cream cakes and laughing.
Clearly, though, none of us love him that much, and
especially not those of us who love his work. We'd
prefer, for his sake, that he could be brilliant with a

large, sophisticated audience whose polish was sufficient to reflect his dazzle but, in lieu of that, we'll settle for brilliant and suffering. There are few people who can suffer as amusingly, revealingly, or fruitfully as Aylett can, nobody with a talent for the torment so they can turn their horror at the ocean of stupidity around them into something at once visionary and disablingly funny. It should also be said that within the field of fantasy and science fiction there are very few creators half as dogged or uncompromising in the pursuit of their muse as is Steve Aylett, or with such good reason.

With the death of William Burroughs, J.G. Ballard mourned the passing of one of the last committed writers, noting that Burroughs' demise had left us only 'career novelists', the ones who had already lined up for the lucrative, blunt-spade accomplished neural surgery as mentioned earlier. These wordsmiths, spayed and tame, know where the grazing land is good and never wander past the stinging cattle-wire of audience comprehension out into the income-threatening wilderness beyond, out into the disreputable pulp-jungles of genre, into art. They know enough to hoard their fuel, dilute the energy to homeopathic doses that will not prove toxic to their audience or sales, to make one second-hand and borrowed concept last a chapter, last for a whole book. Whatever else you do, for God's sake don't burn twenty new ideas with every page as blazing throwaways. That just makes all the other workers on the line look bad, and anyway the constitutions of the readership are for the most part not adapted to ingest raw fire, preferring in the main its faintest after-taste, a water-memory of fire rather than the untreated magma. Aylett, thankfully, has never met or listened to these people, and instead is gloriously unaware which side his bread is buttered. He just keeps on hurtling along, a Porky Pig express train that's dismantling its own box cars to provide the sleepers for the tracks ahead as it roars smoking out amongst the cartoon cacti. When he first emerged in the science fiction field it was into a world of categories and labels that had no idea what to make of him. Was he a cyber-punk, a nano-punk, an Alfred Jarry pata-punk, or just somebody who'd turned up to take the piss? Was this this science fiction comedy, in which case why no punning titles, why no obvious Robert Sheckley retreads, no easy referents, no 'in the grand tradition of…' ? Why weren't there any plots that worked as a three-minute pitch, a three-line jacket blurb? Was he just trying to unsettle everyone?

In fact, Steve Aylett was no kind of literary punk at all. He just liked sunglasses, and that's what had us all confused. If there are any influences to be glimpsed in the almost self-conscious and relentless onslaught of sheer novelty that is his work, they seem to be in influences of an earlier time when there was nothing punk and not much outside *Dr. Who* was cyber; of a period where, when it came to science fiction authors, individual voices were appreciated, and were more than that, demanded. Had he not been born, with perfect Aylett irony, in the Summer of Love, been born too late, he might have had a Michael Moorcock *New Worlds* as a vehicle, have had a context in amongst all of the other brilliant, mismatched oddballs. Aylett is in many ways a staunch traditionalist in that he harks back, ultimately, to the Judith Merrill days when science fiction still had a tradition of originality, before we based our writings on a calculated demographic strategy, when intellectual shock was one of the main reasons that we bothered with science fiction in the first place, and when trilogies of sorcerer-infested fantasy were the exception rather than the norm.

Which brings us to this current volume, *Fain the Sorcerer*, concrete proof that had Steve Aylett launched himself into the marketplace of fantasy rather than that of science fiction, then he would have been no less a marvel nor a prodigy, and he still would have frightened and bewildered us by turn. This is not comic fantasy in the restricted sense the term is used today, the knowing and post-modern slapstick with the title that lampoons a work more widely known, but is instead aggressively inventive, with a comedy that's unrelenting, one of those transcendent satires that ends up a radiant, sublime example of the genre that it's satirising, like Polanski's *Fearless Vampire Hunters*. This is fresh, exciting comic fantasy, but it is also fresh exciting fantasy without whose very ingenuity is his undoing, who has somehow found a scam whereby he can unreel a seemingly unending list of magical abilities which both bewilder and delight. At one point in the narrative Fain backs away dispensing gold coins from one pocket of his coat and sardines from the other, which is an illuminating metaphor for the entirety of Aylett's oeuvre. Read the book, first to yourself, then, unavoidably, aloud to friends until they're sick of you. Hope that Steve Aylett's soul-destroying trail of tears continues if this is an indication of the nuggets that he's finding on the way. Hope also that he one day realizes how ridiculous he is and is delivered in that instant to a lovely maskfaced mermaid, all his endlessly amusing tribulations done. This is a stunning work of the imagination that is also very, very funny, from one of the most exciting and innovative creators to emerge in years. See him, the fabulous self-cursing magus as he backs away, flinging his golden talents and his glittering

192

sardines, each as enticing as the other, offering not only opulence but also salty nourishment. This book, replete with both, is an extravagant and satisfying feast that you should savour, even while resisting the temptation to devour it in a single sitting. Aylett is a jeweler, and this work is one of his most finely chiseled gems. Hold it up to the light and study at your leisure.

Steve Aylett: The Original Source File

Rachel Haywire

Steve Aylett first came to my attention may years ago when I picked up a copy of *Shamanspace,* a book about two rival occult groups in a competition to see who could kill god first. *Shamanspace* was written in a sort of crypto-cyberpunk tongue, which was hilarious and entertaining for me to digest. Being that I ran in similar digital circles, it was all too familiar to me.

Curious to see what Aylett had been up to, I began following him on Twitter. It turned out that he had just released a new book called *Heart of the Original,* which was quite relevant to my interests. I decided to interview him about his recent pursuits.

RH. Let's start with *Shamanspace.* Where did you get the idea to write this book? What inspired it? Was it based in reality?

SA. It makes sense that if god was found to exist and that it was responsible for setting everything up, revenge upon it would be reasonable. If it was woven throughout everything in the universe, then the assassins would constitute its suicide urge, and the universe would end upon termination - a small price to pay.

RH. In your new book *Heart of the Original,* you discuss various ways in which we can revive authenticity in a society that is so utterly manufactured. If you had to sum it up for Trigger Warning readers, what do you think is the best thing we can do to bring forth a resurgence of authenticity?

SA. I summed it up on page 23 of the book in case anyone hadn't twigged by then. "Free of fashion or lobbying, the authentic from-the-ground-up thought of the individual births the original." It's useful not to be stuck to the temporal floor, to not let the times waste your time. Many people find that position incomprehensible or at best unlikely.

RH. In *Heart of the Original* you talk about manufactured surprises. You aptly describe how people wish to have fake surprises handed to them that they already know about. What do you think are the symptoms of this, and do you believe there is anything we freethinkers can do to shift this mass frame of mind?

SA. At its simplest, it's Building Seven Syndrome - just wanting to join in. But at a more harmful level it's about a resistance to learning anything and thus having to do something about what you've learned. Just act surprised by the same thing over and over, announce the same breakthroughs every few decades, and so on. There was a study announced a few weeks ago which showed that *Finnegans Wake* was designed as a fractal. Terence McKenna talked about this (*Surfing on Finnegans Wake*) a few decades ago. I don't know how many times this can be legitimately termed a revelation. I've never used that structure in my books though. After the philosophical parkour of *Heart of the Original* you can hold the whole thing in your head as a mandala or ideogram - the joinery of it's quite precise, including several references to how it works. Anyway at maybe the most toxic level, people participate in mass activities which cause personal or planetary harm at a remove, and it's easy to pretend we're not sharing in the responsibility. I do it too. There's cowardice in numbers. But it shows the ultimate hen-heartedness to be timid of mere new ideas. It's got to the point where people are openly admitting it, as if having no mind or heart of their own isn't something to be ashamed of. I live in the UK, a mean little country which is now devouring itself, but it might be a more general trend. It seems that society, like nature, doesn't like anything which is singular, preferring things which can be reproduced and generalised. But in society and in nature, those singular events are not only the most interesting things going on, they're also the mutations which propel evolution. I don't know whether or not a mass position has to be conscious to qualify as a conspiracy – a lot of things regarded as conspiracy are people having the same idea to move in a certain direction, and being bastards in parallel. The initial resistance to original ideas seems something like that, but when it's so extreme and sustained as at present, exhibiting such fear, the most generous observation can be that it's artificial and consciously directed. Politically induced, in other words. The culture is now so hostile to the authentic, raw origination of ideas it looks downright suspicious. Is freezing evolution a good idea?

RH. Authentic people, as you mentioned, are often scorned by society. Meanwhile our ideas are adapted later, by the same people who previously ostracized us. Is there anything we can do to bypass the scorning and get right to the acceptance, considering that our ideas are going to be adapted by mass culture anyway?

SA. That initial resistance is traditionally a means to disengage a new idea from the person who came up with it, partly so that it can be treated as a notion that just coalesced from all directions and partly to avoid the obligation for gratitude or payment to the actual originator, who will ideally be dead. But beyond this traditional procedure is the more primal fear of true originality, which will find no pre-rendered receptor in the mind because it has never, ever been encountered before. We can have some sympathy for people who are exhausted by work and life and don't have even the small energy available to form a new receptor for the new idea and we can be certain that they will have no sympathy for the exhaustion of those who crave or create such ideas, especially if such original thinkers are their children. It can be especially awkward if a child or adult goes about fomenting common sense while also being creative and imaginative. This can come from a very developed corpus callosum which links the halves of the brain so that imagination and practicality are in communication, da Vinci style. That fuller communication messes up the usual binary stereotypes, presenting onlookers with the nasty prospect of having to think about what's happening. This is all unwelcome in a populace which is mainly just trying to get through the day with a minimum of discomfort. You're treated like a criminal if your mind is the equivalent of a controlled substance. Only you know if you are ready to interact with the world as yourself or as an adjusted avatar. You may not be able to make the moves you need to make if you are beholden. But you know your energy levels and when it's time to hide out. For specific ideas it's worth trying the technique of pretending that a new notion is old so as to make it easier for people to accept - *Heart of the Original* uses that technique from the very first sentence. Credit your idea to someone who lived at least a hundred years ago. It will reassure people that some or all of the acceptance-delay period has elapsed and that it's now okay to think about and use.

RH. How do you feel about censorship and political correctness? Do you think this behavior is a way to weed out dissenting opinions, or do you believe that there is a genuine reason to censor ideas that are considered to be offensive?

SA. I think most people can field and filter their own perceptions but there's nothing wrong with being caring around a friend who you know has a sensitivity to something. No need to be a dick.

RH. Finally, do you plan on writing anything new? What would you like to do in the next few years? Tell us about your future plans.

SA. There are five books in a holding pattern waiting for permission to land but I doubt I'll give permission any time soon. In *Heart of the Original*, I wondered about how long an organism could continue to live if it was constantly putting out energy while receiving nothing back. Could anything keep pouring energy into a vacuum for, say, a couple of decades or more? There is a cute nozzle-mouthed animal called a tardigrade which, when it finds itself in an environment totally hostile to life, goes into complete hibernation, with no detectable life signs, waking again in better conditions. They can exist lifeless for years, as a way of saving their lives. Scientists sent some into space and the tardigrades, sensing that they were trying to thrive in an absolute vacuum, went into total hibernation. That being more or less the situation I find myself in, I'm going to hibernate and be private for several years. When the tardigrades were brought back into a livable environment they came to life again. I don't expect the culture to become more fertile, so the conditions for me publishing again will be personal, not about the environment. Meanwhile I'll be a frightening party clown or some sort of mutant lobster that clings to the side of buildings.

A Steve Aylett Bibliography

NOVELS

The Crime Studio. London: Serif Books, 1994.
Bigot Hall: A Gothic Childhood. London: Serif Books, 1995.
Slaughtermatic. New York: Four Walls Eight Windows, 1997.
The Inflatable Volunteer. London: Weidenfeld & Nicolson, 1999.
Atom. New York: Four Walls Eight Windows, 2000.
Shamanspace. Hove: Codex, 2001.
Only an Alligator. Accomplice Book 1. London: Gollancz, 2001.
The Velocity Gospel. Accomplice Book 2. London: Gollancz, 2002.
Dummyland. Accomplice Book 3. London: Gollancz, 2002.
Karloff's Circus. Accomplice Book 4. London: Gollancz, 2004.
Lint. New York: Thunder's Mouth Press, 2006.
Fain the Sorcerer. Hornsea: PS Publishing, 2006.
The Complete Accomplice. London: Scar Garden Press, 2010.
Novahead. London: Scar Garden Press, 2011.
Rebel at the End of Time. Hornsea: PS Publishing, 2011.

SHORT FICTION

"Infestation." *Carpe Noctem*. Vol 2, Issue 1. 1994.
"Repeater." *TechnoPagan*. London: Pulp Faction, 1995.
"Sampler." *Sex, Drugs, Rock n' Roll: Stories to End the Century*. London: Serpent's Tail, 1997.
"The Passenger." *geek*. 1997. Web.
"The Met Are All for This." *Ethix*. 1997.
"Resenter." *Random Factor*. London: Pulp Faction, 1997.
"Gigantic." *Disco 2000*. London: Sceptre, 1998.
"Tusk." *Fetish*. New York: Four Walls Eight Windows, 1998.
"The Siri Gun." *Crime Time*. Vol. 2, No. 3. February 1998.
"Bestiary." *Gargoyle*. No. 41. June 1998.
"If Armstrong Was Interesting." *Gargoyle*. No. 42. May 1999.
"Shifa." *BritPulp*. London: Sceptre, 1999.
"Download Syndrome." *The Thackery T. Lambshead Pocket Guide to Eccentric and Discredited Diseases*. San Francisco: Night Shade Books, 2003.
"Bossanova." *Quercus SF*. August 2004. Web.
"The Retrial." *Interzone*. No. 198. May-June 2005.
"Stress and Spillover in Three Lint Plays." *Bust Down the Door and Eat All the Chickens*. No. 3. June 2005.
"Whisper." *The Flash: A Flash Fiction Anthology*. London: Social Disease, 2007.
"The Man Whose Head Expanded." *Perverted by Language: Fiction Inspired by the Fall*. London: Serpent's Tail, 2008.
"Voyage of the Iguana." *Fast Ships, Black Sails*. San Francisco: Night Shade Books, 2008.
"Evernemesi." *Beat the Dust*. 2009. Web.
"The Burnished Adventures of Injury Mouse." *Bust Down the Door and Eat All the Chickens*. No. 9. June 2009.

"The Things in the City." *Saucytooth's Webthology*. September 2009. Web.

"Specter's Way." *Crimetime*. June 2010. Web.

"Stingray Valentine." Introduction to *Codename Prague* by D. Harlan Wilson. Bowie: Raw Dog Screaming Press, 2010.

COLLECTIONS

Toxicology. Stories. New York: Four Walls Eight Windows, 1999.

Tao Te Jinx: Collected Quotations of Steve Aylett. Scar Garden Media, 2004.

And Your Point Is? Scorn and Meaning in Jeff Lint's Fiction. Satirical Essays. Bowie: Raw Dog Screaming Press, 2006.

Smithereens. Stories & Essays. London: Scar Garden Media, 2010.

NONFICTION

Heart of the Original. London: Unbound Books, 2015.

COMICS

Tom Strong 27, America's Best Comics, 2004

The Caterer. London: Scar Garden Press, 2005.

Get That Thing Away from Me. Issue 1. London: Scar Garden Media, 2008.

Get That Thing Away from Me. Issue 2. London: Scar Garden Media, 2015.

Johnny Viable & His Terse Friends. Portland, US: Floating World Comics, 2014.

CONTRIBUTORS

BILL ECTRIC wants to believe he can erase the line between science and mysticism. He likes hanging out with other denizens of the burgeoning "Jax by Jax" literary scene in Jacksonville, Florida. Bill's novel, *Tamper*, is about growing up in the 1960s obsessed with unexplained mysteries. The title was inspired by real-life 1940s science fiction writer Richard Shaver, who claimed that underground fiends were *tampering* with his mind. On the internet, Bill's work is featured on Literary Kicks, Sein und Werden, Candlelight Stories, Empty Mirror Books, Spolia, Boston Poetry, Red Fez, Gin Mill Cowboy, The Beat, and Lit Up Magazine.

ROBERT KIELY lectures at Hong Kong Shue Yan University. His publications can be found in *Hix Eros*, *The Parish Review*, *Samuel Beckett Today/Aujourd'hui*, and *Cambridge Literary Review*. He blogs at lithopaedion.blogspot.com.

TONY LEE Writer-editor founded British independent Pigasus Press, and publishes SF, horror stories, and genre poetry, in *Premonitions* magazine (pigasuspress.co.uk), and issued numerous small press 'zines, including *Strange Adventures*, and *FAX 21*. He created nonfiction website *The ZONE* (zone-sf.com), the unique RotaryAction.com - a guide to helicopters in films & TV, and maintains other media outlets VideoVista.net - DVD & blu-ray reviews, and *Soundchecks*.co.uk - for music reviews. For 18 years, Lee reviewed sci-fi and horror books for magazines like *Starburst* and *Shivers* (published by Visual Imagination), before moving on to write columns of DVD & blu-ray reviews for *Interzone* (SF/fantasy), and - until recently -

covered horror films & TV for *Black Static*, both titles published in the UK by TTA Press. Tony's book on Ang Lee's classic 2003 movie *HULK* was published by Telos in 2012. See Tony's blog *Pigasus pressure* at pigasuspress.blogspot.co.uk for more details.

IAIN MATHESON affects himself less than he'd believe: is more relative than absolute. The moments of his life recur, - have never been - save around other people, some of whose valedictions he would envy. One day, perhaps, he'll have been born in Scotland in 1980, and will have studied philosophy at the University of Glasgow, published poems and essays, and been an independent scholar of phenomenology and psychoanalysis.

ALAN MOORE is a legendary English writer known for his work in comic books such as *Watchmen*, *V for Vendetta*, *From Hell*, and *The League of Extraordinary Gentlemen*. In the epic novel *Jerusalem*, Moore channels both the ecstatic visions of William Blake and the theoretical physics of Albert Einstein through the hardscrabble streets and alleys of his hometown of Northampton, UK. In the half a square mile of decay and demolition that was England's Saxon capital, eternity is loitering between the firetrap housing projects.

MICHAEL NORRIS is a freelance writer and tax accountant currently living in Evanston, IL. He has had articles published in *The Paris Times*, *Literary Kicks*, *Live Life Travel*, *Travellers Anonymous*, and other travel and literary sites. Between June 2009 and December 2010, his multi-part exploration of Marcel Proust's *In Search of Lost Time* appeared in *Literary Kicks*, illustrated by David

Richardson. Mr. Norris has had what he calls a chequered career. He worked as a software developer for major corporations and software companies, until moving to Paris, France in 2005. He lived there for four years, working as an ESL (English as Second Language) teacher, and travelling all over Paris teaching English to French business people. During this time he toured extensively in Europe and absorbed the French joie de vivre.

JOHN OAKES is an editor and publisher. Oakes is the co-founder of OR Books, a company recognized by *The Guardian* as one of "the radical alternatives to conventional publishing." He is also publisher of the soon-to-be-revived *Evergreen Review*. Oakes has written for a variety of publications, among them *Publishers Weekly*, the *Review of Contemporary Fiction*, the Associated Press, the *International Herald Tribune*, and *The Journal of Electronic Publishing*. He started his career as a reporter for the Associated Press in New Orleans. In the mid-1980s, Oakes joined Barney Rosset's legendary Grove Press as a junior editor. In 1987, he co-founded an independent publishing company, Four Walls Eight Windows, which he sold in 2004. In 2009, he co-founded OR Books. In 2012, Oakes conceived of and founded the City University of New York (CUNY) Publishing Institute, which he directs. Oakes was named by the French government a Chevalier de l'ordre des arts et des lettres.

SPENCER PATE is a doctoral student in Educational Leadership, Culture, and Curriculum at Miami University in Oxford, Ohio. Spencer has worked as a middle school substitute teacher and as a research assistant at Project Dragonfly, an organization dedicated to inquiry-driven science education and environmental conservation. His academic interests include the philosophy of education, political economy and labor, LGBTQA history, and creative improvisation in classroom teaching. You can find his blog about literature, music, film, and philosophy at lightoflostwords.wordpress.com.

MICHAEL MOORCOCK edited the controversial science fiction magazine *New Worlds* from May 1964 to May 1971. From 1976 through 1996 he was associated with the "new wave" of science fiction in the UK. Moorcock wrote the classic collection of novels and short stories known collectively as *The Dancers at the End of Time* series, set in a future "where entropy is king and the universe has begun collapsing upon itself." His novels about the character Elric of Melniboné were a seminal influence on the fantasy genre in the 1960s and 1970s. In 2008, The Times newspaper included Michael Moorcock in its list of "The fifty greatest British writers since 1945."

ANDREW WENAUS teaches in the Department of English and Writing Studies at Western University and the School of Language and Liberal Studies at Fanshawe College. He has published articles in *Science Fiction Studies*, *Electronic Book Review*, *Extrapolation*, *Foundation*, *The Irish Journal of Gothic and Horror Studies*, *Journal of the Fantastic in the Arts*, *Journal of Popular Music Studies*, and *ESC: English Studies in Canada*. He is currently working on a book-length study that examines expressions of the relationship between programming, information illiteracy, and individual agency in literature after 1945 called *Zero, Zero, and Zero: The Literature of Exclusion*.

RACHEL HAYWIRE is a writer, artist, musician, and model. Recently she founded the INSTED festival, (instedfest.com) which was a counter-TED event for entrepreneurs and artists on the fringes of modern culture. She is also the founder of Trigger Warning, (http://triggerwarning.us) which is a digital platform for dissident and provocative thought. Haywire is a prolific writer; having been featured in the Disinformation anthology "Generation Hex," in addition to authoring the autobiography "Acidexia," and the subversive political writing collection "The New Reaction." She was also the woman behind the industrial music project Experiment Haywire, and created musical compilation "Extreme Women in the Dark Future." Rachel currently lives in San Francisco, CA.

D. HARLAN WILSON is a novelist, short story writer, editor, literary critic, playwright, biographer, and Professor of English at Wright State University-Lake Campus. In addition to over twenty works of fiction and nonfiction, hundreds of his stories and essays have appeared in magazines, journals and anthologies throughout the world in multiple languages. Wilson serves as reviews editor for *Extrapolation*, editor-in-chief of Anti-Oedipus Press, and managing editor of Guide Dog Books. Visit him online at www.dharlanwilson.com.

JIM MATTHEWS has been numerous things in his time (such as a soldier and a graffiti artist) none of which particularly seem to add up. When he has to, he works. It can be anything - teaching English, mixing concrete or drawing pictures. He has published a few short stories and a bit of journalism here and there. He spent 2015 fighting ISIS in Rojava and is working on a book about his experiences there.

RHYS HUGHES has written and published many stories and books in many different languages. He has also written stories and books that have never been published. At the moment, he is working on a weird Western called *The Honeymoon Gorillas*. He is 49 years old.

www.ingramcontent.com/pod-product-compliance
Lightning Source LLC
Chambersburg PA
CBHW051957090426
42741CB00008B/1438